CONTEMPORARY

INTERMEDIATE 2 READER

reading
basics

A REAL-WORLD APPROACH
TO LITERACY

Mc Graw Hill Education

Bothell, WA • Chicago, IL • Columbus, OH • New York, NY

www.mheonline.com

 **Education**

Send all inquiries to:
Contemporary/McGraw-Hill
130 East Randolph Street, Suite 400
Chicago, IL 60601

ISBN: 978-0-07-659102-2
MHID: 0-07-659102-6

Printed in the United States of America.

5 6 7 8 9 QLM 15 14

Contents

UNIT 3

To the Student

The articles in this book will introduce you to some intriguing events, people, and animals. All the articles recount actual events. They are all true stories. They will grab your interest and keep you reading to the end. You will learn something from every article. As you read and enjoy them, you will also develop your reading skills.

You will have many unanswered questions after reading the articles. You may be puzzled or amazed. However, you will not be bored. When you finish reading, you will answer questions to check your understanding of the story. You will also apply critical thinking skills to help you connect to what you have read.

If you finish all 15 lessons—reading the articles and completing the exercises—you will surely increase your reading speed and improve your reading comprehension and critical thinking skills. The exercises include questions similar to those in various assessments. Learning how to complete them will prepare you for tests you may take in the future.

 There is a recording of each article. Go to www.mhereadingbasics.com to play or download the recordings.

The Reading Extension section of the accompanying *Reading Basics Student Edition* relates to the articles. The *Student Edition* presents reading-skill instruction that will help you with your understanding of these articles. You may also read the articles or listen to the recordings any time you wish.

About the Book

Reading Basics Intermediate 2 Reader contains three units, each of which includes five lessons. Each lesson begins with an article about an unusual event, person, group, or animal. A set of six exercises follows each article. The first three reading comprehension exercises will help you better understand the article. These exercises are Recognize and Recall Details, Find the Main Idea, and Summarize and Paraphrase The next three exercises will assist you in thinking about what you have read and how it relates to you own experience. These exercises are Make Inferences, Recognize Author's Effect and Intentions, and Evaluate and Create.

Working through Each Lesson

Begin each lesson by looking at the photograph or illustration and reading the title, the caption, and Before You Read. Next, read the boldface words and their meanings that are in the margins of the article. Then read the article. Finally, complete the exercises. The directions for each exercise will tell you how to mark your answers.

Sometimes your teacher may decide to time your reading. Timing helps you keep track of and increase your reading speed. If you have been timed, enter your reading time in the Timed Reading section at the end of the article. Then use the Words-per-Minute table on page 129 to find your reading speed. Finally record your speed on the Plotting Your Progress: Reading Speed graph on page 130.

Reading Basics will build confidence in your ability to read by letting you practice on short, interesting articles.

King Kong

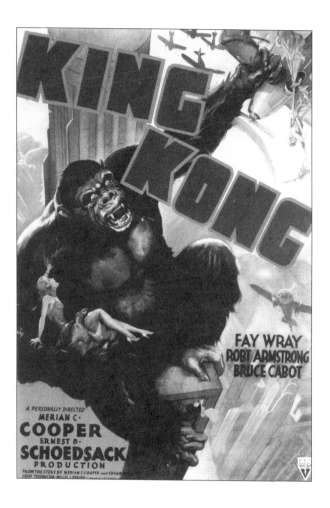

The 1933 movie King Kong *was a huge success. Audiences identified with the giant ape's love for a woman and his fight against those who wanted to kill him.*

Think about what you already know about monsters in movies.

- What do you know about King Kong?
- What are the names of other monsters you have heard of?
- If you have ever seen a monster movie, describe it. Did you feel sorry for the monster? Why or why not?

King Kong

1   The gigantic ape stands atop the Empire State Building in the middle of New York City. In his hand he holds a beautiful woman. Moving gently, he places the woman on a window ledge, the safest spot he can find. Then he turns to bravely face the approaching airplanes. He knows the pilots of the planes are out to kill him, but he will not surrender. After all, he is Kong—King Kong, the most powerful creature ever born.

2   When Kong was living on his own tropical island, he truly was a king. He ruled over every creature in the jungle. Then humans landed on the island. When they discovered the huge ape, they saw not a proud and magnificent creature, but a chance for fame and fortune. They placed Kong in chains and took him to New York, where he was put on public display. People stared at and mocked him. *To mimic as in fun.*

3   Now Kong has broken free from his bonds. He has taken the woman he loves and has climbed to the top of the tallest building in the world, hoping to escape from the men who are trying to recapture him. But as the airplanes move in, Kong sees that there is no escape. The only thing he can do is hold his ground and fight back.

4   When the planes begin their attack, Kong raises one of his giant arms and tries to swat them away. But they move too quickly. Their guns spray a shower of

bullets at Kong and then the planes zoom out of his reach. From the sidewalk below, the people of New York watch as the bullets tear into the gorilla's *huge* — enormous furry body. Again and again the planes swoop in and fire their deadly bursts. Each time, they are able to fly away before Kong can grab them. He swings his arms frantically, trying desperately to fend off his attackers. But when the movie camera zooms in for a close-up, we see that hundreds of bullets have already **pierced** the ape's thick hide. Blood pours from wounds all over his body. It appears that the great Kong has lost the battle.

pierced
penetrated

5 But then, in one swift movement, Kong manages to reach out and grab a plane. As his giant fist closes around it, we hear the crunch of glass and metal. Although we know that there is a pilot trapped inside the airplane, we do not care. We are too caught up in Kong's struggle for survival. We find ourselves rooting for him to destroy the men who are his enemies. When he crushes the airplane and defiantly flings it away, we cheer. For a moment we feel that Kong is once again king.

6 But his triumph is all too brief. Not even the mighty Kong can **withstand** the power of modern weapons. As more and more bullets tear into his body, the great beast weakens and sways. His blood seeps out from the gashes in his body. Finally Kong topples to the pavement far below with a tremendous, earth-shattering thud. Kong's great heart continues to beat for just one more moment before becoming forever still.

withstand
resist

7 So ends the story of King Kong. The movie that portrays the story of King Kong leaves the audience mourning for the fallen ape. And that is exactly what the creator of the movie wanted. His name was Merian C. Cooper. Cooper got the idea for the King Kong movie in 1929 when he was in Africa. He was there to

photograph animals for another film. During his stay, however, he became interested in gorillas. He decided to make a movie about a giant ape with superior intelligence running amok on the streets of a big city.

initially
at first

8 Cooper **initially** intended to film the movie in Africa. But a friend in the movie industry introduced him to a man named Willis O'Brien, who had built many animal models and jungle landscapes for movies. When Cooper saw O'Brien's work, he was greatly impressed. He was so impressed, in fact, that he decided to film *King Kong* in a studio, using O'Brien's models and landscapes.

9 Work on the picture began in 1932. Because it required the use of numerous special effects, it was a difficult and time-consuming movie to make. Cooper had to animate the models of Kong and the other jungle animals. He also had to find a way to animate doll-sized figures of humans that were used in place of actors in some of the scenes. The dolls were used with the Kong model, which was about the size of a person, to make the ape appear gigantic in comparison to humans. In some scenes, for instance, Kong grabbed the tiny "people" in what appeared to be a huge paw. The people models were 16 inches tall and made of rubber and sponge. Kong's shaggy fur was a covering of dyed lambskin. The core of each model was a jointed metal frame. The joints allowed the model to be set in different positions.

10 Action was photographed by shooting a single frame, then moving the joints slightly and taking another picture, and so on. Sometimes a model was moved as little as a quarter of an inch for each shot. It took dozens of such move-and-shoot pictures just to complete a single movement, such as the swinging of an arm or the taking of a step. Although the models

were finely detailed, Cooper felt they weren't quite realistic enough for close shots. So for close-ups he used a huge model of Kong's head and hand, with real actors.

11 It took one year and $650,000 to make *King Kong*. At that time, that was a tremendous amount of money to spend on a film. Most of the money went for special effects, and the investment paid off. When the move-and-shoot pictures were projected on the screen, they looked amazingly lifelike. The close-ups of Kong's head and hand looked so real they were frightening. As word of the movie spread, audiences flocked to movie theaters to see it. The film was so successful that other producers decided to cash in on the theme of sympathetic apes. Eventually there was a whole series of films about giant apes. Among them were *Son of Kong* (1933), *Mighty Joe Young* (1949), *King Kong versus Godzilla* (1962), and *King Kong Escapes* (1967).

12 In 1976, when the original *King Kong* was 43 years old, a new version of the picture was made. The story remained essentially unchanged. The new *King Kong* simply brought the old film up to date. In 1976 the Empire State Building was no longer the tallest building in the world—the twin towers of Manhattan's World Trade Center, which were still standing at the time, were taller. So the new film had Kong climb one of those towers. The remake also replaced the little biplanes that buzzed around Kong with helicopter gunships. The World War I machine guns of the first film became 20-millimeter cannons whose revolving barrels spit thousands of bullets per second.

13 The modern weapons rip bigger, bloodier holes in Kong, but the effect on both ape and audience remains the same. Kong still fights heroically against the deadly weapons of humans. The audience cheers

when Kong grabs and destroys a helicopter that **ventures** too close to his great arms. And of course, in the end, the great Kong collapses and dies.

14   A lot of people who are familiar with the original *King Kong* are disappointed that the new version does not end with the same words as the original. In the first film, as Kong lies dead on the pavement, reporters gather around his body. Carl Denham, the man who captured Kong in the jungle and brought him to New York, also stands over the body. Denham knows that it was Kong's love for the beautiful woman that led to his capture and, **ultimately**, to his death. So as he gazes at Kong's pitiful remains, Denham says, "That's your story, boys. It was Beauty killed the Beast."

15   In many ways, that's what *King Kong* is—the story of beauty and the beast. It is the idea of the beast falling hopelessly in love with the beauty that makes our hearts go out to poor Kong. In the classic story of *Beauty and the Beast*, the hideous beast that loves the beautiful girl turns into a handsome prince in the end. The two then go off together to live happily ever after. In *King Kong*, too, the beautiful woman goes off with a handsome man to live happily ever after. But the man is someone who helped to rescue the woman from the great ape. The poor beast lives on only in the memories of movie fans.

....

Timed Reading

If you have been timed while reading this article, enter your reading time below. Then turn to the Words-per-Minute table on page 129 and look up your reading speed (words per minute). Enter your reading speed on the graph on page 130.

Reading Time: Lesson 1.1

_____ : _____

Minutes   Seconds

COMPREHENSION & CRITICAL THINKING SKILLS

Ⓐ Recognize and Recall Details

Put an **X** in the box next to the answer that correctly completes each statement.

1. In the story, King Kong is captured from his home
   - ☐ **a.** in Polynesia.
   - ☐ **b.** in Africa.
   - ☒ **c.** on an island.

2. Merian Cooper got the inspiration for King Kong while he was in
   - ☐ **a.** Willis O'Brien's studio.
   - ☒ **b.** Africa.
   - ☐ **c.** a zoo.

3. The figure of King Kong was
   - ☐ **a.** a trained gorilla.
   - ☒ **b.** a model of a gorilla.
   - ☐ **c.** a computer image.

4. In the 1976 movie, King Kong grabbed a
   - ☐ **a.** little biplane.
   - ☒ **b.** helicopter gunship.
   - ☐ **c.** space shuttle.

Ⓑ Find the Main Idea

One of the statements below expresses the main idea of the article. One statement is too broad—it is too general. The other statement is too narrow—it explains only part of the article. Label the statements using the following key:

M Main Idea	**B** Too Broad	**N** Too Narrow

_M_   **1.** The movie *King Kong*, which is about a giant ape in love with a woman, is one of the most successful monster movies of all time.

_____   **2.** A remake of *King Kong* in 1976 stuck very close to the original version made in 1933.

_____   **3.** *King Kong* has continued to capture people's hearts and imaginations.

C Summarize and Paraphrase

Put an X in the box next to the answer.

1. Which summary says all the important things about the article?

   ☐ **a.** The 1933 movie *King Kong* led to the creation of a whole series of films about giant apes.

   ☒ **b.** In the 1933 movie *King Kong*, a giant ape is portrayed as a hero who fights to keep the woman he loves. The audience's sympathy for the beast made King Kong one of the best-loved monsters of all times.

   ☐ **c.** In both movie versions about King Kong, the giant ape is portrayed as a hero.

2. The paraphrase below does not say the same thing as the statement. Choose the sentence that best tells why.

   Statement: One reason that audiences sympathized with Kong was that there was a reason for his violent behavior. Kong had been taken from his home and put in chains. Audiences understood Kong's rage.

   Paraphrase: Audiences didn't approve of Kong's violence, but they loved him because of his love for a woman. Many people have been in love, so they understood Kong's feelings.

   ☒ **a.** The paraphrase says too much.

   ☐ **b.** The paraphrase doesn't say enough.

   ☐ **c.** The paraphrase doesn't match the statement.

D Make Inferences

When you combine your own experience with information from a text to draw a conclusion that is not directly stated in the text, you are making an inference. The following inferences about the article may or may not be correct. Label the statements using the following key:

C Correct Inference	**F** Faulty Inference

___F___ **1.** People continue to like *King Kong* because they can relate to the story.

___F___ **2.** The ape movies that followed *King Kong* were very successful.

___C___ **3.** *King Kong* made a lot of money for the studio that produced it.

___C___ **4.** Many monster movies made after 1933 were influenced by *King Kong*.

_____ **5.** People can think of an animal character as if it were a person.

E Recognize Author's Effect and Intentions

Put an X in the box next to the answer.

1. The author uses the first sentence of the article to
   - ☐ **a.** tell about the Empire State Building.
   - ☐ **b.** describe the setting of King Kong's final scene.
   - ☐ **c.** tell the reader how the movie was made.

2. Which of the following statements best describes King Kong?
   - ☐ **a.** "After all, he is Kong— King Kong, the most powerful creature ever born."
   - ☐ **b.** "So for a close-up he used a huge model of Kong's head and hand, with real actors."
   - ☐ **c.** "They placed Kong in chains and took him to New York, where he was put on public display."

3. Choose the statement below that best describes the author's position in paragraph 5.
   - ☐ **a.** Audiences like King Kong because he is a hero.
   - ☐ **b.** King Kong is a monster that has to be stopped.
   - ☐ **c.** The airplane pilot dies a tragic death.

F Evaluate and Create

Put an X in the box next to the answer.

1. Which statement expresses a fact, not an opinion?
   - ☐ **a.** The 1976 version of *King Kong* is better than the original.
   - ☐ **b.** Special effects make movies more enjoyable.
   - ☐ **c.** The Empire State Building is located in New York.

2. Judging from the article, what would have happened if King Kong had been portrayed as a vicious killer?
   - ☐ **a.** He would have won the woman's heart.
   - ☐ **b.** Everyone would have considered him a hero.
   - ☐ **c.** Audiences would not have mourned his death.

3. What is one way a writer can create a movie monster that people sympathize with?
   - ☐ **a.** Show the monster destroying people.
   - ☐ **b.** Show the monster falling hopelessly in love.
   - ☐ **c.** Have the monster climb the world's tallest building.

Nightmare on Chemical Street: The Love Canal Story

Love Canal became a ghost town after people realized that their homes were sitting on the site of a chemical waste dump. Residents asked local, state, and federal governments for help, but it was slow in coming.

Before You Read
Make Connections

Connect what you will be reading to other things you have read or learned.

- What are some poisonous chemicals that people often have in their homes?
- How can families keep their children safe from chemicals in their environment?
- What happens to chemical waste in your area?

1   Imagine that you live in a small, relatively safe neighborhood in a medium-sized city and you walk a short block to your local school. Imagine that you and your friends play in an expansive, grassy field on the weekends. Sounds ideal, doesn't it?

2   That's what Lois and Harry Gibbs envisioned when they bought their house on 101st Street in 1972, and that's also what Barbara and Jim Quimby envisioned when they bought the house Jim had grown up in, just a few blocks away. That's what more than 700 families believed when they moved into the pleasant neighborhood called Love Canal.

3   Love Canal is a section of Niagara Falls, New York. The city has many industries, and most residents work in local plants or factories. Many of the neighbors at Love Canal worked for chemical companies. They didn't make much money at their jobs, but they were proud of their work and wanted a good, safe life for their families. And the pleasant neighborhood provided a great atmosphere in which to bring up children.

4   But in the late 1970s, after several years of heavy rains, people started noticing suspicious things occurring in their homes and on their lawns. Basement walls started oozing thick sludge, and rain puddles glowed bright yellow and purple. Trees and plants began to die, and strong chemical smells wafted through the air all along the streets. And on the wide, grassy field next to the school, corroded metal barrels floated to the surface.

5   Still, most people didn't pay much attention. They were occupied with work or school; they were busy leading normal lives.

6   But in 1978 Lois Gibbs read an article in the Niagara Falls *Gazette* about how the local elementary school had been built on top of a gigantic chemical dump. Lois

was horrified. Her five-year-old son attended that school. He was already experiencing some worrisome problems, and she didn't want them to worsen.

7   Lois did some research on the chemical dump. She had never heard anyone mention it before. She read more newspaper articles and inquired about the canal at the school board and the city government. She couldn't quite believe what her research revealed about the history of Love Canal.

8   The canal was the idea of William T. Love. In 1892 he initiated the construction of a canal to connect two sections of the Niagara River. But he ran out of money, so he abandoned the project. His failed endeavor created the Love Canal—a deep ditch one mile long and 15 yards wide.

toxic
poisonous

9   In the late 1940s the canal was owned by Hooker Chemical Company, which decided to use the old waterway as a dumping site for **toxic** waste. Over the next 11 years, Hooker dumped about 20,000 tons of chemicals into the ditch, and in 1953 the company covered up the barrels of chemicals with dirt. Then it sold the land to the Niagara Falls Board of Education for one dollar.

10   The board of education built a school directly on top of the dirt covering the canal. Then it gave the remaining land to the city. Soon small homes began to appear around the dump site and it seemed that Hooker's chemical graveyard had been forgotten.

11   Lois Gibbs was terrified and furious, because her family was in danger! Usually she was a quiet woman. She had devoted her life to maintaining her home and raising her children, and she hated to speak in public. But she knew something had to be done, so with her neighbors she founded the Love Canal Homeowners Association.

12 Association members confronted the state of New York about the problems at Love Canal. They asked the state to clean up the area, but the state was slow in acting. The Homeowners Association documented the problems, but the government did not believe them.

13 Meanwhile, the homeowners were collecting even more frightening evidence about the dangers of Love Canal. They took a neighborhood health survey and discovered that many residents were suffering from **severe** health problems. There were several people fighting cancer, some children had leukemia or kidney problems, and others had developed mysterious burns or rashes after playing in their yards.

severe
serious

14 In Barbara Quimby's family, everyone was sick. Both Barbara and Jim had spent their entire lives in the neighborhood, and since her childhood, Barbara had suffered from lung problems. When she was in her twenties, doctors had informed her that she had a hernia and an ulcer. She underwent a gallbladder operation. These illnesses are common in elderly people, but they are very rare in a young woman.

15 Jim had terrible problems with migraine headaches, his sister had died of a bone marrow disease when she was only 16, and his father had skin cancer.

16 The Quimbys' eldest daughter was born mentally handicapped and had eye and tooth problems. The youngest daughter had been rushed to the hospital several times with breathing difficulties.

17 But the Quimbys, like most **residents**, couldn't leave Love Canal. As Barbara said, "If we leave here, we'd have to pay rent as well as our mortgage. We have $2,000 in savings, and how long would that last? We hate this house. We really do. But we can't afford a down payment on a new one until we get the money for this one. So we're stuck…"

residents
inhabitants

18   The Love Canal Homeowners Association wanted the U.S. government to declare the area a federal disaster so that New York State would receive enough money to buy the houses around Love Canal.

19   But the state and the federal governments also had pressure from the other side. Some members of the local government didn't want to give Niagara Falls a bad name. The mayor even told the homeowners, "You are hurting Niagara Falls with your **publicity**. There is no problem here."

publicity
attracting
public interest

20   Meanwhile, more worrisome health problems were occurring. In one year, 15 children were born and only two were healthy. The others were born dead or had birth **defects**.

defects
flaws

21   Then the Environmental Protection Agency (EPA) revealed that many residents had suffered from another terrible side effect: tests showed that some people had blood cells that contained broken chromosomes.

22   Chromosomes are small parts of cells and contain information about traits that will be passed on from parent to child.

23   People with broken chromosomes have a higher risk of developing serious illnesses such as cancer, so it's no wonder that people around Love Canal were terrified. They had once believed that the neighborhood was a great place to raise kids, but now they felt as if they were killing their own children. In 1980, after two long years of work, the Love Canal Homeowners Association finally won its battle. The federal government agreed to help New York State buy the homes closest to the dump site and relocate the residents. The decision meant that about 240 families could use the money from the state to purchase new homes in a safer place.

24   But it was too late for many people. Newborn babies had already died, and others had been born

with club feet or extra toes. Some had permanent health problems, such as ulcers or epilepsy, and a few were born mentally handicapped.

25 Adults were dying of cancer or suffering from lung damage. Some people were afraid to have children because they didn't know what their chromosomes would pass on to the next generation.

26 The government made an attempt to clean up the area, but the chemicals were too dangerous to handle and many of them had already leaked into the ground. So Love Canal was covered with a thick layer of clay. Homes that had once edged the grassy field were torn down. The school was closed and the canal was surrounded by a fence.

27 Some houses in the area are still standing. New York state is starting to sell those houses, and once again people are moving into the neighborhood— even former residents.

28 One potential home buyer said, "They must have cleaned Love Canal up pretty well. It's probably one of the safest places to live in Niagara Falls by now."

29 The government hopes it has solved the problems at Love Canal. But rusted barrels of chemicals still lie beneath that layer of clay. Will the tragedy at Love Canal happen all over again?

30 Who knows for sure?

....

If you have been timed while reading this article, enter your reading time below. Then turn to the Words-per-Minute table on page 129 and look up your reading speed (words per minute). Enter your reading speed on the graph on page 130.

Timed Reading

Reading Time: Lesson 1.2   _____ : _____

                                               Minutes   Seconds

Ⓐ Recognize and Recall Details

Put an **X** in the box next to the answer that correctly completes each statement about the article.

1. Who dumped the chemicals into Love Canal?

☐ **a.** Hooker Chemical Company

☐ **b.** William T. Love

☐ **c.** the Niagara Falls Board of Education

2. The Quimby family

☐ **a.** suffered from many serious illnesses.

☐ **b.** worked for Hooker Chemical Company.

☐ **c.** was not concerned about the effects of Love Canal.

3. Chromosomes are parts of cells that

☐ **a.** are not affected by chemicals and toxic waste.

☐ **b.** affected the eating and sleeping habits of the homeowners.

☐ **c.** pass on traits from parents to children.

4. When the government tried to clean up Love Canal, they

☐ **a.** removed all the barrels of chemicals.

☐ **b.** covered the canal with a thick layer of clay.

☐ **c.** destroyed people's memory of the canal.

Ⓑ Find the Main Idea

One of the statements below expresses the main idea of the article. One statement is too broad—it is too general. The other statement is too narrow—it explains only part of the article. Label the statements using the following key:

M Main Idea	**B** Too Broad	**N** Too Narrow

_____ **1.** Chemical dump and toxic-waste sites are very dangerous to people.

_____ **2.** Many residents at Love Canal noticed strange things happening to their homes.

_____ **3.** The chemical dump at Love Canal created serious health and financial problems for the residents.

C Summarize and Paraphrase

1. Look for the important ideas and events in paragraphs 9 and 10. Summarize those paragraphs in one or two sentences.

_____

_____

_____

2. The paraphrase below does not say the same thing as the statement. Choose the sentence that best tells why.

> *Statement*: The Hooker Chemical Company buried their toxic waste in the ditch known as Love Canal. They may not have realized the harmful effects the chemicals would have on future residents of the area.

> *Paraphrase*: The Hooker Chemical Company put a lot of toxic waste in Love Canal.

☐ **a.** The paraphrase says too much.

☐ **b.** The paraphrase doesn't say enough.

☐ **c.** The paraphrase doesn't agree with the statement.

D Make Inferences

When you combine your own experience with information from a text to draw a conclusion that is not directly stated in the text, you are making an inference. The following inferences about the article may or may not be correct. Label the statements using the following key:

C Correct Inference	**F** Faulty Inference

_____ **1.** Hooker Chemical Company did not know about the chemicals in the canal.

_____ **2.** The Quimby family suffered from the effects of the chemicals.

_____ **3.** When the residents of Love Canal complained, the government took immediate action.

_____ **4.** People with broken chromosomes are less likely to have serious health problems.

_____ **5.** A tragedy like the one at Love Canal could happen again wherever people do not know about the dangers of toxic waste.

ⓔ Recognize Author's Effect and Intentions

Put an X in the box next to the answer.

1. Which one of the following statements from the article would the author be most likely to agree with?

   ☐ **a.** Love Canal is a perfectly safe neighborhood now.

   ☐ **b.** The state and federal governments should have acted more quickly to help the residents of Love Canal.

   ☐ **c.** It is not dangerous to build a school on a chemical-waste site.

2. The author says, "Some members of the local government didn't want to give Niagara Falls a bad name." Put an X in the box next to the sentence that has the same meaning.

   ☐ **a.** Some local officials were afraid that bad publicity would ruin the reputation of Niagara Falls as an appealing tourist spot.

   ☐ **b.** Some members objected to changing the area's name.

   ☐ **c.** Some government officials didn't know anything was wrong.

ⓕ Evaluate and Create

Put an X in the box next to the answer.

1. Which one of the following statements from the article is an opinion rather than a fact?

   ☐ **a.** By now we can be sure that Love Canal is one of the nicest places to live in the state of New York.

   ☐ **b.** Love Canal is a section of Niagara Falls, New York.

   ☐ **c.** In the late 1940s, the canal was owned by the Hooker Chemical Company.

2. From what the article said about the cleanup of Love Canal, you can predict that

   ☐ **a.** residents will have no more unusual health problems.

   ☐ **b.** residents will have no more problems of any kind.

   ☐ **c.** residents will continue to have unusual health problems.

3. If you were president of a chemical company, how could you protect the health of people around your business?

   ☐ **a.** Dump toxic waste in a ditch and cover it with dirt.

   ☐ **b.** Sell toxic waste to the government.

   ☐ **c.** Seal chemical waste tightly and store it far away from people.

An Encounter in New Guinea

This scene in the Mumuri village in Papua, New Guinea, is a typical one in the area where Reverend Gill and his staff sighted the UFO.

Before You Read
Clarify

You may need to clarify the meaning of a word, phrase, or abbreviation in order to understand the meaning of a sentence. To clarify the meaning of the term *UFO* in the first paragraph, there are several things you can do:

- Look for familiar words in the article that give a context for the term.

- Continue reading until the meaning of *UFO* becomes clearer.

- Look up *UFO* in a dictionary to see what the letters stand for.

An Encounter in New Guinea

1   What has been referred to as one of the great classics in UFO history occurred on the other side of the world in 1959. The place was a **remote** religious mission on the tropical island of New Guinea, which is located in the Pacific Ocean north of Australia.

remote
out-of-the-way

2   Around 6:45 P.M. on June 26, Reverend William Booth Gill stepped outside the mission to contemplate the evening sky. He located Venus, the brightest star. But what was that surprisingly bright, sparkling object above it? Reverend Gill stared as the sparkling object seemed to descend, and he saw that it was heading straight for the mission!

3   Two of the mission's staff came running at his excited call. Yes, they saw it too. Soon other people from the mission were gazing at the astonishing sight, incredulous.

4   As the object neared, the viewers discerned that it resembled an enormous disk with a wide base and that it had an upper deck with what looked like legs. While the large disk hovered about 300 feet from the ground, small UFOs flew around it. Portholes were visible around the side, and occasionally blue beams were projected into the sky.

5   After observing it for approximately 15 minutes, Reverend Gill thought he noticed movement inside the disk, and he was right. Through the portholes four humanlike figures were visible. They seemed to glow.

transfixed
motionless

6   The dumbfounded group stood by quietly, **transfixed** for about four hours. Then about 11:00 P.M. the disk zoomed away.

7   Having researched UFOs, Reverend Gill was convinced that he had witnessed the visit of a "mother ship," a large spacecraft used as a station for other, smaller craft. He was equally sure that he had seen

aliens inside. Would they return? Gill did not have to wait long for the answer.

8   The next evening the spacecraft was back. It was shortly after sunset, but Gill could see the approaching object quite clearly. Once again he could discern four figures on what was apparently a deck on top of the gigantic disk. "There is no doubt that they were human," he said assuredly. While one of the figures was apparently operating equipment, two others in the central section of the deck were bending over and raising their arms. One of them appeared to be looking down at the men on the ground.

9   Acting on **impulse**, Gill ventured to wave a greeting. To his amazement, the figure waved back! When the others on the ground waved their arms over their heads, the figures on the UFO imitated their gestures! Experimenting further, Gill signaled the craft with an ordinary flashlight. After one or two flashes, the alien disk "wavered back and forth like a pendulum." Said Reverend Gill, "In our estimation there is no doubt that our movements were answered."

impulse
a whim

10   After a while, the figures on the UFO seemed to tire of the game and disappeared below deck, but at 6:25 P.M. they reappeared. Under a blue spotlight, the figures worked on something for five minutes or so. Then Gill made a rather bizarre decision: he and his staff ignored the UFO and proceeded to go inside and eat dinner! Half an hour later they ventured back outside. But by then the UFO had moved a significant distance away, and finally it disappeared entirely from sight.

11   If you had a chance to encounter visitors from outer space, would you wave to them and then proceed to go to dinner? The probability of your making that choice does not seem high. Yet that is exactly what Reverend Gill claims he did.

12   Doubting Gill's story, the Australian Department of Air suggested that the sightings "most probably . . . were reflections on a cloud of a major light source of unknown origin." The Royal Australian Air Force (RAAF) offered another relatively logical explanation: based on "an analysis of bearings and angles above the horizon," the RAAF concluded that "at least three of the lights were planets, perhaps Jupiter, Saturn, and Mars." However, neither of these **theories** is currently considered credible.

theories
guesses

13   As improbable as Reverend Gill's story may be, numerous individuals who talked with him at the time of the event believed he was telling the truth. And in 1977, 18 years later, he still defended his story. But why did he mysteriously choose to have dinner in the midst of one of the most spectacular UFO sightings in history? "We were a bit fed up that they wouldn't come down after all the waving," he explained in a 1977 interview. "This is the difficult thing to get across to people. Here was a flying saucer. Therefore, it must have been a **traumatic** experience. It was nothing of the kind."

traumatic
stressful

14   Many UFO investigators find it difficult to believe that Reverend Gill, a well-educated priest, would make up such a fantastic story just as a hoax. Also in his favor are the 37 other people at the mission who claimed that they too observed the alien objects in the sky. It is hard to dispute a claim that is supported by that many witnesses.

....

Timed Reading

If you have been timed while reading this article, enter your reading time below. Then turn to the Words-per-Minute table on page 129 and look up your reading speed (words per minute). Enter your reading speed on the graph on page 130.

Reading Time: Lesson 1.3   _____ : _____

Minutes   Seconds

COMPREHENSION & CRITICAL THINKING SKILLS

A Recognize and Recall Details

Put an **X** in the box next to the answer that correctly completes
each statement.

1. New Guinea is an island near

   ☐ **a.** Africa.

   ☐ **b.** South America.

   ☐ **c.** Australia.

2. Reverend Gill was in New Guinea

   ☐ **a.** running a religious mission.

   ☐ **b.** taking a short vacation.

   ☐ **c.** investigating reports of UFO sightings.

3. When Reverend Gill waved at the creatures in the UFO, they

   ☐ **a.** landed nearby.

   ☐ **b.** waved back.

   ☐ **c.** sped away in fear.

4. During the second sighting of the UFO, Reverend Gill and his followers

   ☐ **a.** tried to shoot it down.

   ☐ **b.** left to eat dinner.

   ☐ **c.** pleaded with the occupants to go away.

B Find the Main Idea

One of the statements below expresses the main idea of the article. One
statement is too broad—it is too general. The other statement is too
narrow—it explains only part of the article. Label the statements using the
following key:

M Main Idea	**B** Too Broad	**N** Too Narrow

____ **1.** Although experts cannot prove that Reverend Gill actually saw a UFO in
   New Guinea in 1959, many people believe Gill and the eyewitnesses.

____ **2.** In 1959 Reverend William Booth Gill watched and waved to what he
   thought was an alien spacecraft but then took a break for dinner.

____ **3.** UFOs have been reported in many areas of the world.

C Summarize and Paraphrase

1. Reread paragraph 10 in the article. Write a summary of the paragraph in no more than 25 words. Reread your summary and decide whether it covers the important ideas in the paragraph. Then rewrite the summary in 15 words or less without leaving out any essential information.

_____

_____

_____

_____

_____

_____

2. Put an X in the box next to the sentence with the same meaning as the following sentence: "Many UFO investigators find it difficult to believe that Reverend Gill, a well-educated priest, would make up such a fantastic story just as a hoax."

   ☐ **a.** Many UFO investigators believe that Reverend Gill made up his story as a prank.

   ☐ **b.** Many UFO investigators do not believe that a person such as Reverend Gill would tell a false story.

   ☐ **c.** Many UFO investigators think that Reverend Gill's story is wonderful but find it hard to believe.

D Make Inferences

When you combine your own experience with information from a text to draw a conclusion that is not directly stated in the text, you are making an inference. The following inferences about the article may or may not be correct. Label the statements using the following key:

C Correct Inference	**F** Faulty Inference

_____ **1.** Some UFO investigators believe Reverend Gill and the other eyewitnesses.

_____ **2.** The Australian Department of Air believed in the UFO sighting.

_____ **3.** Reverend Gill occasionally acted without thinking.

_____ **4.** Reverend Gill neglected his duties at the mission.

_____ **5.** Reverend Gill had no interest in UFOs or aliens.

E Recognize Author's Effect and Intentions

Put an X in the box next to the answer.

1. The main purpose of the first paragraph is to

   ☐ **a.** compare the UFO encounter in New Guinea with those in other parts of the world.

   ☐ **b.** inform the reader about the exact location of New Guinea.

   ☐ **c.** describe the setting of a classic UFO sighting.

2. Choose the statement that best describes the author's position in paragraph 11.

   ☐ **a.** Reverend Gill's actions prove that he is not telling the truth.

   ☐ **b.** It is not likely that someone would have dinner while a UFO is present.

   ☐ **c.** Reverend Gill was afraid of his visitors.

3. The author tells this story mainly by

   ☐ **a.** retelling Reverend Gill's experiences with a UFO.

   ☐ **b.** comparing Reverend Gill's experiences with those of others who have seen UFOs.

   ☐ **c.** telling different stories about UFO sightings in New Guinea.

F Evaluate and Create

Put an X in the box next to the answer.

1. You can predict that if the UFO had started to come down, Reverend Gill

   ☐ **a.** would not have left to have dinner.

   ☐ **b.** still would have left to have dinner.

   ☐ **c.** would have left but not had dinner.

2. What was the effect when Reverend Gill's signaled the craft with a flashlight?

   ☐ **a.** The visitors disappeared below deck.

   ☐ **b.** The disk wavered back and forth.

   ☐ **c.** The visitors waved to him.

3. If you were a UFO investigator, how could you use the information in the article to study UFOs?

   ☐ **a.** I could try to communicate with UFOs using light beams.

   ☐ **b.** I could make sure I ate dinner before any creatures from outer space visited me.

   ☐ **c.** I could establish a religious mission in New Guinea.

Ocean-born Mary

For years, stories have circulated of strange happenings at this house in Henniker, New Hampshire, known as the Ocean-born Mary house.

Before You Read
Use Prior Knowledge

You already know about many things from your own life experience. Making a connection between what you already know and what you are reading makes it easier to learn and remember new material. Ask yourself:

- What ghost stories have I read or heard?
- What ghost stories can I share with others?

1   In the town of Henniker, New Hampshire, stands a grand old house with a fascinating legend attached to it—a legend that some people would like to erase and others insist on preserving. For generations, stories have circulated of eerie happenings in and around the house. It has been said that sometimes awful groans of a dying man can be heard in the woods behind the house. Strangest of all, every now and then at dusk a coach drawn by four horses has reportedly taken shape at the front door. Inside the coach sits a tall woman with flaming red hair. It is the ghost of Ocean-born Mary, and this house once belonged to her.

2   The story of Ocean-born Mary begins in Londonderry, Ireland, in 1720. A ship full of people in search of a new life in the New World was setting sail for Boston. Among those on board were James Wilson and his wife, Elizabeth, who was soon to bear their first child. They were bound for Londonderry, New Hampshire.

3   On July 28 Elizabeth gave birth to her child. At about the same time as the child was born, one of the ship's lookouts sighted land—America! Right after, another lookout, perched high atop the mainmast, spotted another ship and shouted, "Sail ho!"

4   The captain knew that his ship was easy prey for pirates. Then the strange vessel drew nearer, fired its cannon, and broke out the skull and crossbones. Two rowboats were lowered over the side of the pirate ship. A group of fierce-looking men **brandishing** swords and pistols rowed swiftly to the immigrant ship and clambered onto its deck. At their head was a tall, dark-skinned man called Pedro. "Lash the men together!" he ordered. "Once we get the valuables, we'll kill them all!"

brandishing
waving

5   Pedro himself went below deck to search for valuables. He soon found what he was looking for: chests containing silver, gold, and jewels. As he ran his hands through the treasure, he heard a whimper.

He drew his pistol and followed the sound down a passageway to a locked cabin door. Pedro crashed through the door and discovered a terrified Elizabeth Wilson. She was lying in bed, her newborn baby cradled in her arms.

6   "Is it a girl?" Pedro asked gently. "Yes," Elizabeth whispered. "Has she been named yet?" Pedro inquired.

hesitant
uncertain

"No… not yet," came Elizabeth's **hesitant** reply.

7   "My dear," he said to Elizabeth, "if you give this child my mother's name, I swear I will not harm this ship nor any of its passengers." A bewildered Elizabeth nodded yes. "Her name shall be Mary," Pedro said and quickly left the cabin.

8   Back on deck, Pedro shouted a series of commands to his men. "Return the treasure! Release the men! We are leaving this vessel!"

9   In a short time, Pedro returned to Elizabeth's cabin carrying a package in his arms. Thrusting the bundle at her, he said, "This is for little Mary's wedding dress." Pedro then returned to his own ship and sailed away. Inside the package, Elizabeth found a bolt of pale green silk embroidered with flowers.

10   Soon after the immigrant ship landed safely in Boston, James Wilson died. Elizabeth and her baby daughter went on to Londonderry, where a piece of land awaited them. The story of the newborn child who had saved a ship spread quickly. Everyone began calling her "Ocean-born Mary."

11   The years passed, and Mary grew up to be a beautiful, bright-eyed, red-haired woman nearly six feet tall. When she married, she wore a wedding dress of green silk embroidered with flowers.

12   All the facts up to this point are of historical record. Here the legend begins. Mary and her husband, James

Wallace, lived in Londonderry and had four sons. When the children were still very young, Mary's husband died. The pirate Pedro had never forgotten the baby girl he had named for his mother. Hearing that Mary was widowed, Pedro decided to help. He went to Henniker, New Hampshire, and built a great house deep in the woods. Then Pedro sought out Mary.

13   Mary had long been curious about the pirate who had named her. She was happy to meet him. She found him to be both kindly and generous. "Care for me in my old age," Pedro said to Mary, "and I will see that you and your sons **lack** nothing." Mary agreed and moved to Henniker to live in Pedro's house.

lack
do without

14   Then one day Pedro left for the seacoast. When he returned he was accompanied by a pirate. The two men carried a huge chest, which they lugged deep into the woods and buried. When the last shovelful of earth had been thrown, a cry was heard in the night. Pedro returned from the woods, but his companion was not with him. The companion was never seen again.

15   Months after this incident, Mary returned from a drive in her coach to find the house empty. Where was Pedro? She found him behind the house, dead, his heart pierced by a cutlass. Pedro's body was buried under the huge hearthstone in the kitchen of the great house.

16   Mary stayed on in the house Pedro had built for her until her death in 1814, at the age of 94. According to legend, Mary's ghost visits the house, usually around sunset.

17   In recent years the legend has **distressed** the people who live in the house. They claim there is no ghost.

distressed
upset

18   The house, which has come to be called the Ocean-born Mary House, wasn't Mary's at all. It was built by Mary's son Robert. Mary never lived there.

19   Historical records show that Mary and James had four sons and a daughter. The records also show that Mary's husband did not die until he was 81 years old. Mary was 71 at the time. If Pedro had still been alive at that time, he would have been approximately 100 years old. He never bought any land in Henniker or searched for Mary Wallace.

20   In 1798, when she was 78 years old, Mary left Londonderry to live with her son William in Henniker. She lived in William's home until her death. Mary's grave, in the cemetery behind the Henniker Town Hall, is marked by a slate headstone. Inscribed are the words, "In Memory of Widow Mary Wallace who died Feb. 13, 1814, in the 94th year of her age."

21   How did such a wild legend happen? It was all part of a moneymaking scheme. In 1917 a man named Louis Roy purchased the Robert Wallace house. Then he created the story about Mary and Pedro, the buried treasure, the cries in the woods, and the ghost. Newspapers and magazines spread the story. Mr. Roy gave tours of the house for an admission fee and rented shovels for 50 cents apiece, so that visitors could dig for the buried treasure.

plagued
tormented

22   The legend of Ocean-born Mary has been proved to be false. But some people just refuse to believe the facts. The family that bought the house is still **plagued** by people wanting to see the ghost. A good ghost story dies hard.

....

Timed Reading

If you have been timed while reading this article, enter your reading time below. Then turn to the Words-per-Minute table on page 129 and look up your reading speed (words per minute). Enter your reading speed on the graph on page 130.

Reading Time: Lesson 1.4   _____ : _____

                                  Minutes   Seconds

Ⓐ Recognize and Recall Details

Put an **X** in the box next to the answer that correctly completes each statement.

1. The story of Ocean-born Mary takes place mainly

   ☐ **a.** in Ireland.

   ☐ **b.** in New Hampshire.

   ☐ **c.** on board a ship.

2. Pedro gave Elizabeth a bundle that contained

   ☐ **a.** a bolt of cloth.

   ☐ **b.** the treasure his men had collected.

   ☐ **c.** his mother's wedding gown.

3. In reality, Mary Wallace lived most of her life in

   ☐ **a.** Boston, Massachusetts.

   ☐ **b.** Londonderry, New Hampshire.

   ☐ **c.** Henniker, New Hampshire.

4. In the legend, Ocean-born Mary had

   ☐ **a.** two sons and no daughters.

   ☐ **b.** four sons and no daughters.

   ☐ **c.** four sons and a daughter.

5. In reality, Mary Wallace had

   ☐ **a.** two sons and no daughters.

   ☐ **b.** four sons and no daughters.

   ☐ **c.** four sons and a daughter.

Ⓑ Find the Main Idea

One of the statements below expresses the main idea of the article. One statement is too broad—it is too general. The other statement is too narrow—it explains only part of the article. Label the statements using the following key:

M Main Idea	**B** Too Broad	**N** Too Narrow

____ **1.** The story of Ocean-born Mary has captured people's imaginations for generations.

____ **2.** Ocean-born Mary was born at sea and named by a pirate.

____ **3.** Ocean-born Mary was a real historical figure around whom a fantastic legend was woven involving a pirate and buried treasure.

C Summarize and Paraphrase

1. Reread paragraph 20 in the article. Write a summary of the paragraph in no more than 25 words. Reread your summary and decide whether it covers the important ideas in the paragraph. Then decide how to shorten the summary to 15 words or less without leaving out any essential information.

_____

_____

_____

_____

_____

_____

2. Read the statement about the article below. Then read the paraphrase of that statement. Choose the reason that best tells why the paraphrase does not say the same thing as the statement.

   Statement: The legend presents Mary as a young widow who met Pedro, but in reality Mary was married until she was 71 and never met Pedro.

   Paraphrase: Mary and Pedro never actually met.

   ☐ **a.** Paraphrase says too much.

   ☐ **b.** Paraphrase doesn't say enough.

   ☐ **c.** Paraphrase doesn't agree with the statement about the article.

D Make Inferences

When you combine your own experience with information from a text to draw a conclusion that is not directly stated in the text, you are making an inference. The following inferences about the article may or may not be correct. Label the statements using the following key:

C Correct Inference	**F** Faulty Inference

_____ **1.** Immediately after Pedro spared the ship on which Mary was born, he gave up pirating.

_____ **2.** The real Mary Wallace hoped that she would get to meet Captain Pedro.

_____ **3.** Pedro loved his mother.

_____ **4.** Mary Wallace actually led a pretty ordinary life.

_____ **5.** Mary's son Robert did not want his mother in his house.

ⓔ Recognize Author's Effect and Intentions

Put an X in the box next to the answer.

1. The author uses the first sentence of the article to

   ☐ **a.** express a criticism of the Ocean-born Mary legend.

   ☐ **b.** introduce the debate over the Ocean-born Mary legend.

   ☐ **c.** compare the Ocean-born Mary legend to other ghost legends from Henniker, New Hampshire.

2. In paragraph 12, "Here the legend begins" means

   ☐ **a.** the following story is probably true, but there is no hard evidence to prove it.

   ☐ **b.** the story that follows is absolutely true.

   ☐ **c.** the story that follows is probably not true.

ⓕ Evaluate and Create

Put an X in the box next to the answer.

1. From what the article said about the legend of Ocean-born Mary, you can predict that

   ☐ **a.** many people will continue to believe the fake story.

   ☐ **b.** everyone will stop believing the fake story.

   ☐ **c.** Mary and Pedro will continue to haunt the Robert Wallace house.

2. What was the cause of Pedro's decision to leave the immigrant ship and its passengers unharmed?

   ☐ **a.** Elizabeth Wilson agreed to make Mary a wedding dress of green silk.

   ☐ **b.** Mary Wallace agreed to care for Pedro in his old age.

   ☐ **c.** Elizabeth Wilson agreed to name her newborn baby Mary.

3. Into which of the following theme categories would this story belong?

   ☐ **a.** Everyone—even a murderous pirate—is basically good.

   ☐ **b.** Almost everyone loves a good ghost story.

   ☐ **c.** Some people will do anything for money.

4. In which paragraph did you find the information or details to answer question 2?

   ☐ **a.** paragraph 5

   ☐ **b.** paragraph 7

   ☐ **c.** paragraph 9

Custer's Last Stand: Battle of Little Bighorn

The Battle of Little Bighorn took place in Montana on June 25, 1876. This romanticized 1889 lithograph depicts the battle.

Before You Read
Preview

Previewing an article is a good way to prepare for reading.
To preview an article:

- Read the title and the caption and look at the illustration.

- Skim the text to get a general idea of what the article is about.

- Go to the end of the article and read the questions. As you read, look for information that helps answer these questions.

1   The June sun glared down on Lieutenant Colonel Custer and his 225 weary soldiers. Time was running out, and Custer knew that their only chance for survival was to charge the hill in front of them. Behind them, Chief Gall and 1,500 warriors were already attacking.

2   Custer may have paused to glance up at the crest of the hill and see what awaited him. Crazy Horse and at least 1,000 warriors had reached the crest before him. The Sioux and Cheyenne had the Seventh Cavalry surrounded.

3   As the smoke from the guns and the clouds of churning dust cleared, only a few white men remained standing. Dead and dying men and horses covered the slope near the Little Bighorn River. Custer was one of the few troopers still on his feet, but within 20 minutes the battle would be over and Custer and every soldier with him would be dead.

4   Probably no other battle in the history of the United States has generated more controversy than the Battle of Little Bighorn, or "Custer's Last Stand." Why did Custer suffer such a crushing defeat?

5   George Armstrong Custer had always wanted to be a soldier. In 1861 he graduated last in his class from West Point. But during the Civil War he quickly proved that he was a fearless leader. By the age of 25 he was made a major general.

6   Many of those who served with the "boy general" in the war thought that he was a brave man. Yet many others **resented** his flashy style and felt that he was a proud, **overbearing** "glory hunter." Custer often disobeyed orders and, instead of the standard army uniform, he often wore a fringed buckskin suit.

resented
were offended by

overbearing
bossy

7   But when the Civil War ended, the army no longer required as many generals. Custer was demoted in

rank to lieutenant colonel. He was assigned second-in-command of the newly formed Seventh Cavalry.

8   The tasks of the army were to protect the crews of workers building the railroads in the West and to deal with the Plains Indians. In 1874 Custer ventured into the Black Hills for an **exploratory** trip. After surveying the area, Custer sent a scout back to the fort with an extraordinary news release: Gold in the Black Hills! However, years earlier, the federal government and the Sioux had negotiated a treaty giving the Sioux ownership of that land. No one could use the land if the Sioux did not grant them permission.

exploratory
fact-finding

9   But the desire for gold proved too strong to deter. In less than a year, thousands of miners and their families poured into the region. The government approached the Sioux to negotiate a sale of their territory.

10   The Sioux refused to sell. They banded together with the Cheyenne near the Little Bighorn River. In their vast camp of thousands of men, women, and children, there were at least 3,000 warriors. Custer was eager to battle the Sioux and Cheyenne because he felt that a victory was the only way to **restore** his damaged reputation with President Ulysses S. Grant. Custer had served under the president during the war but had recently angered him. Grant's brother had been involved in a scandal, and Custer had testified against him. An enraged Grant took away Custer's command.

restore
rebuild

11   At last Custer's friend, Major General Alfred Terry, persuaded Grant to let Custer rejoin the Seventh Cavalry at Fort Abraham Lincoln in what is now North Dakota. Although Grant agreed, he insisted that Terry be in command. Custer and the Seventh were now in Terry's force. Their job was to locate the Sioux-Cheyenne camp.

12   In June 1876 Terry's forces were to meet with those of Colonel Gibbon and General Crook, but their forces were attacked along the way and were unable to join Terry. At that point, Terry gave Custer strict orders to lead the Seventh to the Little Bighorn valley and *wait* for Terry and the others to join him.

13   Custer wanted to make sure that he would get the glory of defeating the Plains Indians. He and the Seventh made a forced march to the Little Bighorn River, riding late into the night each night and starting again before dawn. Custer arrived at the designated meeting place well before schedule.

14   Even though Terry had ordered Custer to do nothing until the others arrived, Custer had no intention of waiting. His scouts warned him that the Sioux camp they found was larger than any they'd ever seen before, but Custer ignored their warnings and decided to attack.

15   Then Custer made another **devastating** mistake. He divided his already outnumbered Seventh Cavalry. He told Captain Frederick Benteen to take 125 men and sweep south of the river valley, and Major Marcus Reno was given 140 men and told by Custer, "Take your battalion and try to bring them to battle, and I will support you with the whole outfit."

devastating
disastrous

16   Why did Custer divide his troops? Did he realize what he was asking of Reno? He was sending Reno to attack the south end of what was probably the largest group of Plains Indians ever to assemble.

17   Custer and his 225 men galloped into the ravine toward the Indian camp. In the meantime, Reno and his men were under attack, waiting for Custer to join them. Reno was a capable officer, but neither he nor his tired men had any experience fighting the Indians.

The warriors outnumbered the soldiers and had better weapons. The soldiers carried single-shot rifles, but the Indians had the latest Winchester repeaters.

18   After 20 minutes of fighting, Reno reluctantly ordered a retreat. Benteen met up with Reno. Neither command could reach Custer because they were driven back by the Sioux.

19   Custer and his men were trapped. They were outnumbered by more than 10 to 1. Most of the troopers' rifles jammed, which meant the soldiers had to use knives to dig the cases from the chambers and then reload. The Indians kept up a steady stream of weapon fire. As the ranks of soldiers thinned, the Sioux and Cheyenne moved in and killed the remaining troops with knives and hatchets. The Sioux and the Cheyenne, directed by Sitting Bull, Crazy Horse, and Gall, did not relent until Custer and all 225 of his men were dead. The lone survivor was a horse named Comanche. After the attack, the Seventh Cavalry made sure that the badly wounded Comanche was returned to the fort, and he became a symbol of the Battle of Little Bighorn.

20   Many feel that Custer lost the now-famous battle but was part of the overall "victory" that involved the confiscation of Indian land. Soon after Custer's defeat, the Plains Indians were forced to sell their land and move onto reservations.

Timed Reading

If you have been timed while reading this article, enter your reading time below. Then turn to the Words-per-Minute table on page 129 and look up your reading speed (words per minute). Enter your reading speed on the graph on page 130.

Reading Time: Lesson 1.5

_____ : _____

Minutes   Seconds

COMPREHENSION & CRITICAL THINKING SKILLS

Ⓐ Recognize and Recall Details

Put an **X** in the box next to the answer that correctly completes each statement about the article.

1. Custer had fought in the
   - ☐ **a.** Civil War.
   - ☐ **b.** Mexican War.
   - ☐ **c.** American Revolution.

2. Custer's cavalry included Captain Benteen and
   - ☐ **a.** Colonel Gibbon.
   - ☐ **b.** Major Marcus Reno.
   - ☐ **c.** Major General Alfred Terry.

3. When Reno's command began to lose the fight, they
   - ☐ **a.** went back to the fort.
   - ☐ **b.** retreated.
   - ☐ **c.** surrendered.

4. The Battle of Little Bighorn occurred in
   - ☐ **a.** September 1875.
   - ☐ **b.** May 1861.
   - ☐ **c.** June 1876.

5. The Seventh Cavalry was equipped with
   - ☐ **a.** single-shot rifles.
   - ☐ **b.** Winchester repeaters.
   - ☐ **c.** knives.

Ⓑ Find the Main Idea

One of the statements below expresses the main idea of the article. One statement is too broad—it is too general. The other statement is too narrow—it explains only part of the article. Label the statements using the following key:

M Main Idea	**B** Too Broad	**N** Too Narrow

_____ 1. In 1876 a Sioux-Cheyenne force completely wiped out Custer and the 225 men of the Seventh Cavalry near the Little Bighorn River.

_____ 2. Custer's defeat has been a subject of interest to historians for years.

_____ 3. At least 3,000 Sioux and Cheyenne warriors were camped at Little Bighorn.

C Summarize and Paraphrase

Put an X in the box next to the answer.

1. Which summary says all the most important things about the article but in the fewest words?

    ☐ **a.** Custer lost the Battle of Little Bighorn. Custer and all of his men were killed in the battle.

    ☐ **b.** Eager to defeat the Sioux and Cheyenne at the Battle of Little Bighorn, Custer made a series of mistakes that led to his defeat. Custer and all of his men were killed.

    ☐ **c.** Custer wanted to fight the Sioux and Cheyenne at the Battle of Little Bighorn because he wanted to restore his reputation with President Grant. However, after Custer divided his troops, he was hopelessly outnumbered by the strong Indian force. Custer, and all 225 of his men were killed in the battle.

2. Choose the sentence with the same meaning as this sentence: "Most of the troopers' rifles jammed, which meant the soldiers had to use knives to dig the cases from the chambers and then reload."

    ☐ **a.** Because their rifles jammed, most of the soldiers had to use knives to fight the Indians while they reloaded.

    ☐ **b.** Before they could reload, the soldiers had to use knives to fix their rifles.

    ☐ **c.** Before they could reload their rifles, the soldiers had to use knives to dig their ammunition out of the ground.

D Make Inferences

When you combine your own experience with information from a text to draw a conclusion that is not directly stated in the text, you are making an inference. The following inferences about the article may or may not be correct. Label the statements using the following key:

C Correct Inference	**F** Faulty Inference

____ **1.** Custer will not be remembered for his skilled leadership.

____ **2.** The Seventh Cavalry used old rifles and ammunition.

____ **3.** Major General Terry disliked Custer.

____ **4.** The Sioux and Cheyenne cared more about the gold than their land.

E ⬤ Recognize Author's Effect and Intentions

Put an X in the box next to the answer.

1. Which of these statements from the article best describes Custer's personality?

   ☐ **a.** George Armstrong Custer always wanted to be a soldier.

   ☐ **b.** In 1861 he graduated last in his class from West Point.

   ☐ **c.** Yet many others felt he was a proud, overbearing "glory hunter."

2. The author probably wrote this article in order to

   ☐ **a.** express a negative opinion of Custer.

   ☐ **b.** compare Custer's soldiers to the Indian warriors.

   ☐ **c.** tell the reader about Custer and the Battle of the Little Bighorn.

3. The author's purpose for writing paragraph 15 was to

   ☐ **a.** tell the reader that lots of Sioux were prepared to fight at Little Bighorn.

   ☐ **b.** suggest that Custer had no concern for his troops.

   ☐ **c.** tell the reader about some mistakes Custer made.

F ⬤ Evaluate and Create

Put an X in the box next to the answer.

1. Which of these statements is an opinion rather than a fact?

   ☐ **a.** No other battle in the history of the United States was more exciting than the Battle of Little Bighorn.

   ☐ **b.** By the age of 25 Custer had been made a brigadier general.

   ☐ **c.** The only survivor of the battle was a horse named Comanche.

2. From what the article told about the U.S. government's treatment of the Sioux, you can predict that

   ☐ **a.** the government respected the wishes of Native Americans.

   ☐ **b.** Native Americans came to trust the government.

   ☐ **c.** the government valued the wishes of non-Native people over those of Native Americans.

3. Into which theme category would this story fit?

   ☐ **a.** The desire for wealth is the root of all evil.

   ☐ **b.** Too much pride can lead to a downfall.

   ☐ **c.** Violence is not an effective way to settle differences.

Kim's Story: The Big Bubble

This artist's interpretation is similar to the UFO that Kimberly Baker stated she saw. She said it looked like a shiny bubble and that there was a man with it.

Before You Read
Predict

One way you can get more from what you read is to make a reasoned guess about what you think will happen in an article and then check to see whether it happened. Predict what the author will say in this article based on:

- the title.
- the photo.
- the photo caption.

1   Richard Bonenfant, an investigator of unidentified flying objects (UFOs), headed for the town of Bingham, Maine, as soon as he heard the news. He had a hunch that it would be worth investigating.

2   *BINGHAM—She's just six years old but states she saw a UFO on the afternoon of April 23, and nobody has been able to "shake" her story. Of course, Kimberly Baker doesn't call it a UFO or a flying saucer. To her it looked like a "big ball" or a "bubble."*

3   The article appeared in the *Morning Sentinel* of Waterville, Maine. According to the article, the field in which Kimberly reported the sighting "appeared as if some object might have landed on it, for grass and close-to-ground greenery were flattened."

4   Bonenfant wondered if Kimberly would prove to be a reliable witness, or if her story was merely a **figment of her imagination**. The following account is based on Richard Bonenfant's report.

figment of her imagination
something she invented

5   According to Kim, on April 23, 1966, she and her two cousins, Wendy and Bruce, had walked to a field near her cousins' house to pick pussy willows. When they discovered the stems were too strong to break off by hand, Wendy and Bruce headed back to their house for a pair of scissors. While Kimberly waited for her cousins to return, she observed a large, shiny object floating toward her. Too frightened to move, she watched as the object landed a few yards away. For more than a minute Kimberly stared at the object, expecting something—anything—to happen. Instead, it suddenly rose into the air and flew away, disappearing over the roof of a neighbor's house, as quickly and silently as it had arrived.

6   When the little girl returned home later that day, she tried to tell her mother what she had seen.

7　"Mommy, Mommy, I saw something!" Kimberly shouted excitedly, tugging at her mother's skirt.

8　But Mrs. Baker was preoccupied that afternoon and didn't pay much attention to her daughter's pleadings. Two days later, though, Mrs. Baker remembered Kimberly's excitement and stopped to ask her daughter about it.

9　"What did you see?" asked Mrs. Baker.

10　Kimberly said she had seen "a big bubble," and went on to describe the size and color of the "bubble." It was "like Daddy's car but higher," she said, adding that it was "shiny, like the toaster in the kitchen." In answering her mother's questions, Kimberly revealed that the object also had a door and a rectangular-shaped window about eight inches high, a flashing green light fixed just above the center of the object, and red lights at either end. Asked if she'd be able to draw a picture of the object, Kimberly **readily** complied.

readily
willingly;
without effort

11　Mrs. Baker didn't think her daughter's experience was some fantasy she had invented, but she wasn't certain what to do. Finally she called on a family friend, Allie King, who worked for the Gannett Publishing Company, which owned several newspapers.

12　On April 27, Allie King questioned Kimberly about the experience. Although King repeatedly tried to confuse the young girl, Kimberly never once **wavered** from her story. During King's questioning, however, Kimberly revealed something quite unexpected.

wavered
shifted away

13　"Were you afraid when you saw the bubble?" Kimberly was asked.

14　"At first I was," she answered, "but not after the man smiled at me."

15 Allie King and Mrs. Baker were startled by that statement. This was the first time Kimberly mentioned a man in connection with the sighting. Mrs. Baker tried to conceal the nervousness in her voice.

16 "What did the man look like, Kimberly?" she asked.

17 Kimberly said the man was dressed in "shiny white" with "lots of black buttons on his chest," and resembled her father, or a family friend named René. After removing what appeared to be a "bubble" on his head, the man winked, smiled, and moved his lips as if he were trying to say something; however, no sounds came forth.

18 Kimberly then led her mother and Allie King to the location in the field where the craft had landed. Even days later, a circular area of flattened grass about 15 feet in diameter was still clearly visible. Within the circle, pussy willow stems had been broken off. Instead of their usual whitish-yellow color, these stems were dark, as if they had been burned.

19 Impressed by Kimberly's story and by the evidence in the field, Allie King contacted a reporter from the *Morning Sentinel*. On May 4, reporter Richard Plummer interviewed Kimberly. The details of Kim's account were consistent with her earlier statements. However, Mrs. Baker was in for another surprise when she asked her daughter if anyone else had seen the "bubble."

20 "Yes," Kim answered. "A dog saw it, and he barked, too!"

21 Later a neighbor confirmed that a mongrel had created quite a **din** the Saturday afternoon of

din
loud noise

Kimberly's sighting, but the neighbor had ignored the dog's **incessant** barking.

22   Did Kimberly Baker have an encounter with a UFO? After talking at length with her and visiting the landing site himself, Bonenfant concluded that Kimberly was a reliable witness, and that what she observed was not a conventional aircraft. His evaluation of the sighting—UNKNOWN— demonstrates that he felt what Kimberly saw wasn't of this Earth.

Timed Reading

If you have been timed while reading this article, enter your reading time below. Then turn to the Words-per-Minute table on page 129 and look up your reading speed (words per minute). Enter your reading speed on the graph on page 130.

Reading Time: Lesson 2.1

_____ : _____

Minutes   Seconds

A Recognize and Recall Details

Put an **X** in the box next to the answer that correctly completes each statement about the article.

1. The *Morning Sentinel* was the name of a
   - ☐ **a.** book written about Kimberly Baker.
   - ☐ **b.** newspaper in Waterville, Maine.
   - ☐ **c.** story written about a UFO encounter.

2. When Kimberly first saw the object floating toward her, she
   - ☐ **a.** cried out in excitement.
   - ☐ **b.** was afraid.
   - ☐ **c.** ran home to her mother.

3. Mrs. Baker thought her daughter's story was
   - ☐ **a.** made up.
   - ☐ **b.** not a fantasy.
   - ☐ **c.** told to Kimberly by her cousins.

4. Allie King
   - ☐ **a.** taught school.
   - ☐ **b.** was a local TV news anchor.
   - ☐ **c.** worked for the Gannett Publishing Company.

5. In the end, Kimberly's story
   - ☐ **a.** turned out to be false.
   - ☐ **b.** had changed many times in the telling.
   - ☐ **c.** was believed by several people.

B Find the Main Idea

One of the statements below expresses the main idea of the article. One statement is too broad—it is too general. The other statement is too narrow—it explains only part of the article. Label the statements using the following key:

M Main Idea	**B** Too Broad	**N** Too Narrow

_____ 1. Many UFO sightings have been reported in the United States.

_____ 2. A UFO investigator and a reporter believe that Kimberly Baker experienced a UFO encounter.

_____ 3. Kimberly Baker told her mother she saw a "bubble" land in a field near her cousins' house.

C Summarize and Paraphrase

1. Reread paragraph 5 in the article. Write a summary of it in 25 words or less on the lines below. Reread your summary and decide whether it covers the important ideas in the paragraph. Then decide how to shorten the summary to 15 words or less without leaving out any essential information.

_____

_____

_____

_____

_____

2. Choose the best paraphrase for this sentence from the article:

"Later a neighbor confirmed that a mongrel had created quite a din the Saturday afternoon of Kimberly's sighting, but the neighbor had ignored the dog's incessant barking."

☐ **a.** The neighbor hadn't been aware of the dog's barking the Saturday afternoon that Kimberly saw the UFO.

☐ **b.** The neighbor said that a dog had indeed made a lot of noise that Saturday, but the neighbor had ignored it.

☐ **c.** The neighbor said that the alien had made a lot of noise that Saturday, so the neighbor had paid no attention to the dog.

D Make Inferences

When you combine your own experience with information from a text to draw a conclusion that is not directly stated in the text, you are making an inference. The following inferences about the article may or may not be correct. Label the statements using the following key:

C Correct Inference	**F** Faulty Inference

_____ **1.** Kimberly Baker liked to make up stories.

_____ **2.** Kimberly and her cousins were friends.

_____ **3.** Mrs. Baker rarely paid attention to her daughter.

_____ **4.** Kimberly was an observant child.

_____ **5.** Richard Bonenfant was impressed with Kimberly.

E Recognize Author's Effect and Intentions

Put an **X** in the box next to the answer.

1. The author uses the first sentence of the article to

   ☐ **a.** make the reader curious.

   ☐ **b.** describe typical UFO investigation tactics.

   ☐ **c.** express an opinion about UFO investigators.

2. Judging by the statement "Mrs. Baker didn't think her daughter's experience was some fantasy she had invented," the author wants the reader to think that

   ☐ **a.** Mrs. Baker did not usually believe Kimberly's stories.

   ☐ **b.** Kimberly had no imagination.

   ☐ **c.** Kimberly's account of the experience was believable.

3. The author probably wrote this article in order to

   ☐ **a.** tell the reader about Kim's encounter with the "bubble."

   ☐ **b.** convince the reader that Kim had a UFO encounter.

   ☐ **c.** entertain the reader with a child's fantasy.

F Evaluate and Create

Put an **X** in the box next to the answer.

1. Choose the statement that expresses an opinion.

   ☐ **a.** A circular area of flattened grass was still visible.

   ☐ **b.** A dog barked on the day of Kim's sighting.

   ☐ **c.** Kim was a brave and intelligent little girl.

2. Choose the letter of the phrase that correctly completes the following statement: In the article, what Kim saw and _____ are alike.

   ☐ **a.** what Wendy saw

   ☐ **b.** what Mrs. Baker did

   ☐ **c.** the cause of the dog's barking

3. What did you have to do to answer question 2?

   ☐ **a.** find an opinion (what someone thinks about something)

   ☐ **b.** find a cause (why something happened)

   ☐ **c.** make a comparison (how things are the same)

Poison on the Drugstore Shelf

After the deadly Tylenol poisonings in Chicago in 1982, employees of the Chicago City Health Department tested the medication for the presence of cyanide.

You may want to clarify certain aspects of an article. For example, given the title and caption of this article, you might be confused about whether or not it is still dangerous to take Tylenol. To clarify, you can:

- skim the article for facts and dates.
- check other sources if you find that the article does not provide enough information.

1   Early one morning in October 1982 Adam Janus, age 27, awoke with a pain in his chest. The pain wasn't too severe, but it was significant enough to bother him. He went out to a local store and purchased a bottle of Extra-Strength Tylenol capsules. He returned to his house in Arlington Heights, Illinois, where he swallowed at least one capsule. An hour later he collapsed. His family rushed him to the hospital, watching in horror as doctors struggled in vain to revive him. Adam's heart and lungs had stopped working. Dr. Thomas Kim, one of the doctors who had attempted to save Adam, was shocked at the young man's death. "He suffered sudden death without warning," said Dr. Kim. "It was most unusual."

2   Adam's family was overwhelmed by his unexpected death. That evening they gathered together at the Janus home. No one was feeling very well, and someone offered to buy a bottle of aspirin. But Stanley Janus, Adam's younger brother, pointed out the bottle of Tylenol in the kitchen. He and his wife, Theresa, each took at least one capsule. Five hours after his older brother's death, Stanley Janus was pronounced dead. Theresa died two days later.

3   In nearby Elk Grove Village, 12-year-old Mary Kellerman, who was suffering from a cold, took a

Tylenol and died. Mary Reiner of Winfield, who had recently returned from the hospital with her new baby, also took a Tylenol and died suddenly. Paula Prince, a flight attendant, was found dead in her apartment in Chicago. In the bathroom was an open bottle of Tylenol.

4   By the end of the week, seven people in the Chicago area had died after taking Tylenol. It was discovered that each person had swallowed a capsule loaded with cyanide (SYE-uh-nide), an extremely dangerous poison.

5   Apparently, the killer had taken apart several Tylenol capsules. Then he or she had inserted huge quantities of cyanide into the red portion of the capsules before putting them back together again. After adding the poison, the killer had returned the **contaminated** bottles of medicine to store shelves. As Winfield's police chief said, "Apparently a very sophisticated and very **malicious** person is at large who had to spend a lot of time and effort on this terrible plan."

contaminated
poisoned

malicious
spiteful

6   Even though the seven victims all resided in the Chicago area, the poisonings caused panic across the country. Cyanide in drugstore medicine! Who would die next? Johnson & Johnson, the company that manufactures Tylenol, stopped all production and asked store owners to remove the capsules from their shelves. Police stations and hospitals were overrun with people convinced they had been poisoned. One Chicago hospital received 700 calls in a single day. Dr. William Robertson, director of the Poison Control Center in Seattle, had some advice for callers. He said, "If it was going to be a lethal dose, you wouldn't have time to call."

7   The Illinois attorney general began a nationwide search for the killer. Police all over the country investigated old and new cases, hoping to find a promising lead. In California, Pennsylvania, and Wyoming, they found similar poisoning cases, but some were clearly unrelated and others were "copycat" cases set up by people interested in attention.

8   Still, the copycat killers were dangerous in their own right. As Halloween approached, some cities and towns prohibited trick-or-treating. Citizens were afraid that children would be hurt. And in fact, three children in Chicago got sick after eating chocolate bars. People were afraid to buy anything from the store. Food and drug manufacturers began to realize that they needed to make safer packages in order to remain in business.

9   In mid-October a letter arrived at the office of McNeil Consumer Products, the branch of Johnson & Johnson that manufactures Tylenol. The author of the letter threatened more poisonings unless the company sent $1 million to a mailbox at a Chicago bank.

10   The extortion letter was eventually linked to James and LeAnn Lewis—also known as Robert and Nancy Richardson. FBI agents soon learned about James Lewis's frightening past. Kansas City police recognized him as a tax accountant who was once charged in the killing of an elderly man. He was also accused of attacking his mother with an axe, and he had been hospitalized twice for mental health problems. In 1974 his five-year-old daughter had died after heart surgery, and a police officer who knew Lewis claimed he had always blamed Johnson & Johnson for his daughter's death.

11 But when the FBI entered the Lewises' apartment in Chicago, they found no trace of the couple. They tracked the pair to New York City, where more than 100 FBI agents searched for them.

alias
a fake name

12 In November the *Chicago Tribune* received a letter signed by Robert Richardson—an **alias** frequently used by James Lewis. The letter said, "My wife and I have not committed the Chicago-area Tylenol murders." Records showing that the Lewises had been in New York when the tainted Tylenol first appeared on shelves in Chicago supported Lewis's claim.

extort
blackmail

convicted
found guilty

13 James Lewis was finally arrested in December 1982 when a librarian at a branch of the New York Public Library recognized his face and called the police. He went to trial, accused of trying to **extort** money from Johnson & Johnson. Lewis was eventually **convicted** of that charge and sentenced to 20 years in prison. He was paroled in 1995 and moved to the Boston area. Although he was never charged with the Tylenol murders, the parole commission was not convinced he was innocent. In February 2009 FBI agents took boxes and a computer from Lewis's condo in Cambridge, Massachusetts. The FBI said it was the result of new forensic advancements and new tips. So far, the new evidence has not led to an arrest.

14 This tragedy changed the ways in which food and medicine are packaged. Bottles and boxes now have special safety seals, and pills are often enclosed in individual plastic packs.

15 Still, better packaging does not guarantee safety. In 1986 Diane Elsroth bought a bottle of Tylenol. Minutes later she was dead, killed by cyanide that

had been inserted into the capsules. The brand-new package had three separate safety seals. However, the killer had somehow managed to get past those seals and add poison to the capsules.

16 In the end, there is nothing anyone can do to make packages completely safe. But food and drug companies are doing their best to make sure that their products are as tamper-proof as possible.

....

If you have been timed while reading this article, enter your reading time below. Then turn to the Words-per-Minute table on page 129 and look up your reading speed (words per minute). Enter your reading speed on the graph on page 130.

Timed Reading

Reading Time: Lesson 2.2

_____ : _____

Minutes   Seconds

(A) Recognize and Recall Details

Put an **X** in the box next to the answer that correctly completes each statement about the article.

1. The first Tylenol deaths took place in
   - ☐ **a.** 1986.
   - ☐ **b.** 1982.
   - ☐ **c.** 1963.

2. The seven people who died all lived in
   - ☐ **a.** the Seattle suburbs.
   - ☐ **b.** California, Pennsylvania, or Wyoming.
   - ☐ **c.** the Chicago area.

3. James Lewis was convicted of
   - ☐ **a.** trying to extort money from Johnson & Johnson.
   - ☐ **b.** murdering at least seven people.
   - ☐ **c.** stealing manufacturing secrets from Johnson & Johnson.

4. Lewis also used the alias
   - ☐ **a.** Robert Richardson.
   - ☐ **b.** James Smith.
   - ☐ **c.** Ralph Anderson.

5. Because of the Tylenol scare, food and drug companies
   - ☐ **a.** stopped making painkillers.
   - ☐ **b.** made packaging safer.
   - ☐ **c.** boycotted Johnson & Johnson products.

(B) Find the Main Idea

One of the statements below expresses the main idea of the article. One statement is too broad—it is too general. The other statement is too narrow—it explains only part of the article. Label the statements using the following key:

M Main Idea	**B** Too Broad	**N** Too Narrow

_____ **1.** Adam Janus bought contaminated Tylenol at a local store.

_____ **2.** Several people died after a killer put cyanide into Tylenol capsules.

_____ **3.** Contaminated food and drugs caused a nationwide panic.

◉ Summarize and Paraphrase

1. Look for the important ideas and events in paragraphs 1 and 2. In your notebook, summarize those paragraphs in one or two sentences.

2. Complete the following one-sentence summary of the article using all three phrases from the phrase bank below. Write the letters on the lines.

> **Phrase Bank:**
>
> **a.** the cause of those deaths
>
> **b.** several mysterious deaths in the Chicago area
>
> **c.** the search for the killer and efforts to improve packaging

The article about the Tylenol tampering scare begins with _____, goes on to explain _____, and ends with _____.

3. Put an X in the box next to the best one-sentence paraphrase of this sentence from the article: "James Lewis was finally arrested in December 1982 when a librarian at a branch of the New York Public Library recognized his face and called the police."

☐ **a.** A librarian in a New York library recognized Lewis and had him arrested.

☐ **b.** A librarian in New York City arrested Lewis in December.

☐ **c.** A librarian from a New York library thought that James Lewis's face looked familiar.

◉ Make Inferences

When you combine your own experience with information from a text to draw a conclusion that is not directly stated in the text, you are making an inference. The following inferences about the article may or may not be correct. Label the statements using the following key:

> **C** Correct Inference   **F** Faulty Inference

____ **1.** The Janus family suffered a terrible tragedy.

____ **2.** The Tylenol killer was a careful, intelligent person.

____ **3.** The copycat cases did not worry the police.

____ **4.** The FBI had no trouble tracking down the Lewis couple.

____ **5.** The Tylenol case influenced the packaging of other products.

E Recognize Author's Effect and Intentions

Put an **X** in the box next to the answer.

1. What is the author's purpose in writing "Poison on the Drugstore Shelf"?

    ☐ **a.** to encourage the reader not to use any medicine

    ☐ **b.** to inform the reader about the Tylenol scare in the 1980s

    ☐ **c.** to convey a mood of fear

2. How is the author's purpose supported in paragraph 15?

    ☐ **a.** The author inspires fear of all drugstore medicine.

    ☐ **b.** The author believes that packaging for medicine is never totally safe.

    ☐ **c.** The author tells the reader about another case of Tylenol poisoning.

F Evaluate and Create

1. Put an X in the box next to the sentence that best predicts something that will probably happen in the future.

    ☐ **a.** Food and drug companies will eliminate tamper-proof seals because they do not guarantee safety.

    ☐ **b.** Food and drug companies will continue to take steps to make their products safe.

    ☐ **c.** The production of Tylenol will be halted.

2. Put an X next to the phrase that correctly completes the following statement.

    On the positive side, bottles and boxes now have special safety seals, but on the negative side, _____.

    ☐ **a.** James Lewis was arrested.

    ☐ **b.** copycat crimes occurred after the Tylenol murders.

    ☐ **c.** poison was added to Tylenol capsules enclosed in a sealed box.

3. Fill in the blanks in the cause-effect chart using statements a, b, and c. Write the letters on the lines.

    a. James Lewis was recognized.

    b. Drug companies now try to make their products tamper-proof.

    c. He died.

CAUSE	EFFECT
Adam Janus took a Tylenol capsule.	_____
Tylenol was tainted with cyanide.	_____
_____	He was arrested.

Death on the Unsinkable Titanic

"Sinking of the Titanic" by Willy Stoewer shows the ship just before it sank. The watertight compartments could not keep the ship afloat, as many of them had been damaged by the iceberg that the ship hit. People in the lifeboats could see the hundreds of passengers aboard the ship left to their fate.

When you don't know much about a topic, you can look for information about it before you read. For this article, for example, you can:

- do research in the library or on the Internet to find information about the sinking of the *Titanic*.

- discuss the movie *Titanic* with classmates.

Death on the Unsinkable Titanic

1   "The safest ship afloat." "A seagoing hotel!" "Unsinkable!" These were the descriptions that writers used in newspaper articles about the *Titanic*, the largest ship ever constructed at that time.

2   In April 1912 the *Titanic* was sailing from Southampton, England, to New York City on its first voyage. The captain of the British ship was E. J. Smith, a veteran of many years of transatlantic service. Smith wanted to prove that the *Titanic* was not only the world's most **luxurious** ship but also the fastest. To achieve that goal, Smith held the *Titanic* to a speedy 22 knots for the majority of the voyage.

luxurious
rich and splendid

3   The *Titanic* was equipped with the very latest wireless equipment, which it used to communicate with other ships. The *Titanic's* wireless operators had received warnings from two neighboring ships that they had seen several icebergs, but in spite of the warnings, Captain Smith maintained a speed of 22 knots.

4   One of the ship's lookouts, Fred Fleet, peered ahead from his position high atop the mast. In the distance he spotted a huge bulk looming in *Titanic's* path—an iceberg! Fleet struck three bells—the signal for something dead ahead. First Officer Murdoch, on watch on the bridge, ordered the ship to turn *hard-a-starboard*. At almost the same instant, Murdoch

signaled the engine room to stop. The *Titanic* began to turn to one side, as if in slow motion, but it was too late. With a long, grinding sound, the *Titanic* scraped along the side of the iceberg. The passengers barely felt the impact because the blow was a glancing one; it was almost a near miss. Pieces of ice rained down on one of the *Titanic's* decks, but the passengers, in a holiday mood, felt no sense of danger. After all, everyone knew the *Titanic* was unsinkable. Besides, it had been a minor collision. Card players continued their games. Some passengers sent waiters to pick up chunks of ice from the deck to use to cool their drinks.

5   Below decks in the engine room, however, the crew could see that the damage to the *Titanic* was severe. The iceberg had ripped a long, jagged gash below the vessel's waterline, and the sea was pouring in.

6   The *Titanic* consisted of 16 watertight compartments that divided the ship into sections from bow to stern. It had been designed so that if any compartment suffered a hole, doors would close and isolate that section. The undamaged compartments would be more than sufficient to keep the ship afloat. In fact, if the *Titanic* had collided with the iceberg head on, the damage would have been much less significant. At worst, the bow and the first couple of watertight compartments would have sustained damage. When the *Titanic* turned to avoid the iceberg, however, a jagged underwater spur of ice scraped along its hull, creating a 300-foot wound in the *Titanic's* side. Water was pouring into too many of the compartments for the ship to remain afloat.

7   In approximately 10 minutes, the depth of the water in the forward compartments was eight feet. Though the ship's pumps had been activated, they were ineffective. Below in the fire rooms, sweating

stokers shoveled coal into the great furnaces of the *Titanic's* boilers. Those boilers supplied power for the pumps and provided electricity for the lights and the wireless.

8   The engineers and stokers were fighting a losing battle, however, as water was flooding in much too quickly for the pumps. Slowly, the engine room crew retreated before the steadily advancing water. Although many of the boilers were flooded out, enough kept functioning to furnish electricity for the ship's lights and the wireless equipment. This enabled the crew of the *Titanic* to send an SOS.

9   Another ship, the *Carpathia*, received the *Titanic's* SOS, but it was hours away. In response to the SOS, the *Carpathia* doubled the number of stokers feeding its furnaces and sent a wireless message to the *Titanic*: "Coming hard!"

abandon
leave

10   *Titanic's* captain gave the order to **abandon** ship. The old rule of the sea—women and children first— was sounded; however, not many passengers responded to the command. People simply didn't believe that the *Titanic*, with its double bottom and watertight compartments, could sink. Many wives refused to be separated from their husbands. As a result, the first lifeboats pulled away from the ship only half filled.

11   The sinking *Titanic* was bathed in the glow of distress rockets that were fired every few minutes. Passengers began to understand that the impossible was actually happening. The *Titanic* was going down! The lifeboats were now heavily loaded. And when people realized there wouldn't be nearly enough room in the boats for all of them, they began to panic.

12   The *Titanic's* massive bow sank deep under water, causing its stern to rise slowly into the air. The screws—those gigantic propellers that had driven the ship toward a new speed record and toward disaster—were swinging up. Finally they were entirely pulled out of the water.

13   People in the lifeboats could see, by the glare of the *Titanic's* remaining lights, the hundreds of passengers left to their fate aboard the ship. The occupants of the lifeboats watched with a grim **fascination**. They could see their doomed relatives and friends aboard the now rapidly sinking ship. Then the tremendous ship gave a final shudder, stood on end, and plunged beneath the sea.

fascination
strong attraction

14   The lifeboats had moved away from the *Titanic* in order to avoid being pulled down by the suction created by the giant ship as it sank. The occupants of the lifeboats **assessed** their situation. The *Titanic* had been carrying over 2,200 passengers and crew members. The lifeboats had a capacity of 1,178. However, as a result of the confusion and people's disbelief that the ship would actually sink, only 711 people had **secured** places in the lifeboats.

assessed
took stock of

secured
obtained

15   Approximately 20 minutes after the *Titanic* had vanished under the sea, the *Carpathia* arrived on the scene in response to the *Titanic's* SOS. The *Carpathia's* searchlight probed the night expecting to find the great ship; however, the beams of light picked up only small lifeboats—some all but empty—bobbing about on the sea. The unsinkable *Titanic* had carried over 1,500 people with it to a watery grave. The *Carpathia* took the 711 survivors aboard. Then the liner headed for New York at its best speed.

16   The *Titanic* and the passengers and crew members it carried lay undisturbed beneath the sea for approximately three quarters of a century. Over those long years, many expeditions searched for the remains of the *Titanic*. In 1986 Alvin, a midget submarine designed for deep-water exploration, joined the search. *Alvin* succeeded in locating the *Titanic's* rusty remains. The vessel lay in two pieces, more than two and one-half miles below the water's surface. The ship's bow had plunged 50 feet into the muddy bottom before settling down into the sand. The rear portion of the ship, badly broken up, lay some distance away. Scattered about the wreckage for some distance were reminders of the passengers it had carried. *Alvin's* video cameras captured images of champagne bottles, china cups and saucers, and the head of a little girl's doll lying on the ocean floor.

17   The crew of the midget submarine placed a bronze tablet near the *Titanic's* stern in memory of the 1,522 souls who perished with the great ship.

Timed Reading

If you have been timed while reading this article, enter your reading time below. Then turn to the Words-per-Minute table on page 129 and look up your reading speed (words per minute). Enter your reading speed on the graph on page 130.

Reading Time: Lesson 2.3

_____ : _____

Minutes   Seconds

Ⓐ Recognize and Recall Details

Put an X in the box next to the answer that correctly completes each statement about the article.

1. The *Titanic* was speeding along at 22 knots because

    ☐ **a.** the captain wanted to prove it was the world's fastest ship.

    ☐ **b.** the crew was unaware that there were icebergs nearby.

    ☐ **c.** it was running late.

2. The *Titanic* may not have had as much damage if

    ☐ **a.** it had not swerved to avoid the iceberg.

    ☐ **b.** there had been lookouts on duty.

    ☐ **c.** it had carried wireless equipment.

3. The iceberg

    ☐ **a.** crushed the *Titanic's* bow and first compartments.

    ☐ **b.** crushed the *Titanic's* stern.

    ☐ **c.** slashed open many of the *Titanic's* watertight compartments.

4. The *Titanic's* pumps

    ☐ **a.** were too small for such a large ship.

    ☐ **b.** couldn't keep up with the huge amounts of water pouring in.

    ☐ **c.** were out of order.

Ⓑ Find the Main Idea

One of the statements below expresses the main idea of the article. One statement is too broad—it is too general. The other statement is too narrow—it explains only part of the article. Label the statements using the following key:

M Main Idea	**B** Too Broad	**N** Too Narrow

_____ **1.** Icebergs can do tremendous damage to ships.

_____ **2.** Over 1,500 people died when the *Titanic* sank after hitting an iceberg.

_____ **3.** An iceberg slashed a 300-foot gash in the *Titanic's* side.

C Summarize and Paraphrase

1. Look for the important ideas and events in paragraphs 13 and 14. Summarize these paragraphs in one or two sentences.

_____

_____

_____

_____

2. Read the statement about the article below. Then read the paraphrase of that statement. Choose the reason that best tells why the paraphrase does not say the same thing as the statement. Put an X in the box next to the answer.

   Statement: *Alvin's* video cameras captured images of champagne bottles, china cups and saucers, and the head of a little girl's doll lying on the ocean floor.

   Paraphrase: *Alvin* used its video cameras to photograph the *Titanic*.

   ☐ **a.** The paraphrase says too much.

   ☐ **b.** The paraphrase doesn't say enough.

   ☐ **c.** The paraphrase doesn't agree with the statement about the article.

D Make Inferences

When you combine your own experience with information from a text to draw a conclusion that is not directly stated in the text, you are making an inference. The following inferences about the article may or may not be correct. Label the statements using the following key:

C Correct Inference	**F** Faulty Inference

_____ **1.** The *Titanic* should not have been traveling so fast.

_____ **2.** The engineers and the stokers couldn't believe that the *Titanic* was going to sink.

_____ **3.** Passengers showed good judgment when they refused to leave in the first lifeboats.

_____ **4.** Captain Smith felt very proud of the *Titanic* and was also very confident of its strength.

_____ **5.** The rescuing ship, *Carpathia*, expected to arrive before the *Titanic* sank.

E Recognize Author's Effect and Intentions

Put an X in the box next to the answer.

1. Which of the following statements from the article best describes the way engineers had constructed the *Titanic* to be sure it would stay afloat?

   ☐ **a.** "The *Titanic* carried the very latest in wireless equipment."

   ☐ **b.** "After all, everyone knew the *Titanic* was unsinkable."

   ☐ **c.** "It had been designed so that if any compartment suffered a hole, doors would close and isolate that section."

2. From the statement "but in spite of the warnings, Captain Smith maintained a speed of 22 knots," you can conclude that the author wants the reader to think that

   ☐ **a.** the *Titanic* was the fastest ship in the world.

   ☐ **b.** Captain Smith was reckless and didn't want anything to slow down the *Titanic*.

   ☐ **c.** 22 knots was not very fast.

3. The author tells this story mainly by

   ☐ **a.** comparing the *Titanic* to the *Carpathia*.

   ☐ **b.** describing the passengers and crew of the *Titanic*.

   ☐ **c.** describing how the passengers and crew reacted to the disaster.

F Evaluate and Create

Put an X in the box next to the answer.

1. Choose from the letters below to correctly complete the following statement.

   The article states that the only people who were saved were

   ☐ **a.** those who were picked up by the *Carpathia*.

   ☐ **b.** the stokers.

   ☐ **c.** the crew.

2. What was the effect of the passengers' reluctance to get in the lifeboats?

   ☐ **a.** Fewer people were saved.

   ☐ **b.** The *Titanic* sank faster than normal because of the extra weight of the people who stayed on board

   ☐ **c.** All the lifeboats left without taking any passengers.

Sarah's Ghost House: An Architectural Fun House

Sarah Winchester, an eccentric heiress, built a maze of rooms to keep pursuing ghosts away. She believed that as long as she continued to build on to the house, she would remain alive and unharmed. In the end, the house covered six acres and contained 160 rooms.

Previewing the lesson gives you an idea of what you are going to read. To preview the lesson, you can:

- look at the photograph.

- read the title of the article and the photo caption.

- skim the article to get an idea of the way it is organized.

- read the questions after the article. As you read the article, you can look for information that will help you answer the questions.

1   In 1862 Sarah Pardee married William Wirt Winchester, heir to the Winchester rifle fortune. (At that time the Winchester rifle was the most famous rifle in the world.) Sarah and her husband moved to a large, lovely home in New Haven, Connecticut. Soon Sarah gave birth to a baby girl, whom they named Annie Pardee. Sarah seemed to have everything to look forward to; however, just one month later tragedy struck. Baby Annie died from a mysterious illness, and a few short months later, William also died.

2   Sarah was devastated by this double tragedy. She withdrew into her home, refused to see anyone, and became convinced that the Winchesters were cursed. The rifle that bore their name had been responsible for the deaths of thousands. Sarah believed that the spirits of those who had been killed were seeking revenge.

3   Sarah had always been intrigued by the occult— the mysteries of the spirit world—but now she became **obsessed** with it. Hoping to make contact with her deceased daughter and husband, Sarah invited mediums into her home. Mediums claim that they can contact the dead through meetings called séances. None of the mediums Sarah met with, however, were able to make a connection with William or with baby Annie.

obsessed
totally absorbed

4   Then Sarah learned of a medium named Adam Coons, who lived in Boston, Massachusetts. People assured her that if it were possible to make contact with the dead, Coons would be the one who could do it. Without identifying herself, Sarah visited Coons, and he agreed to stage a séance for her.

5   During the séance, Coons informed Sarah that the spirit of her late husband was standing beside her. "Tell him that I miss him desperately," she said. "He wants you to know that he will always be with you," Coons replied. Then he gave Sarah a chilling warning. "Unless you do something in their memory, the ghosts of those who have been killed by Winchester rifles will haunt you forever."

6   "But what can I do?" Sarah pleaded. Coons instructed her to move to the West and purchase a house that her husband's spirit would pick out. Then she was to enlarge the house, making sure it had sufficient room to house the spirits of those killed by Winchester rifles. As long as she continued to build onto the house, Coons assured Sarah, she would remain alive and unharmed.

7   Coons hadn't known Sarah's identity. How, then, had he known about her husband's death and the family's connection to the Winchester rifle? Sarah was convinced that her husband's ghost had spoken through the medium. She set out to follow his instructions.

8   In 1884 Sarah sold her home in New Haven and traveled west to California. There, following what she later said was William's advice, she purchased an eight-room house on 44 acres of land in San Jose, a city approximately 50 miles south of San Francisco.

9   She immediately set about increasing the size of the house. Fortunately, money wasn't a problem.

Sarah had not only inherited William's fortune—approximately $20 million—she also received about $1,000 a day from the Winchester Arms Company.

10   A small army of workers was in Sarah's constant employ. There were 18 carpenters, 12 gardeners, and countless plumbers, plasterers, stonemasons, and painters. For the next 38 years, they worked around the clock, every day, all year long. The hammering and sawing never ceased.

11   Sarah herself took control of every detail of the work. Each morning she presented the head workman with the plans she had sketched on an old envelope or paper bag the previous evening. And each night she'd seek the opinions of the ghosts that she believed inhabited the house. More often than not, it seems, the spirits didn't like Sarah's plans, or they'd change their minds about what they wanted.

12   As a result, walls constructed one day would be torn down the next. Windows would be installed only to be blocked up. Doors were added, then removed, and so on. One worker spent 33 years repeatedly laying fancy wooden floors and then tearing them up!

13   As each new room was completed, Sarah would furnish it or fill it with treasures that she'd later use to furnish additional rooms. There were rooms that held rolls of costly French wallpapers; stacks of paintings; or ornaments of copper, gold, and silver.

14   Railroad cars filled with European and Asian riches for Sarah's mansion arrived almost daily at the San Jose depot. For small items, Sarah shopped locally. She'd drive one of her two automobiles—both two-tone lavender and yellow Pierce Arrows—into town, but when she arrived at a store, she never

exited the car. No matter, for the eager shopkeepers gladly brought items out for her approval.

15   Sarah spent almost as much time planning the grounds around the house as she did the house itself. She ordered her gardeners to plant a six-foot-high cypress hedge around the perimeter of the entire estate. She also had them plant exotic gardens and orchards. In one of the gardens, a statue that **depicted** Chief Little Fawn shooting arrows was sculpted to honor the many Native Americans killed by white armies using Winchester rifles. Elaborate fountains **spewed** water 24 hours a day and several paths wound through this wonderland in a confusing maze.

depicted
pictured

spewed
shot forth

16   In the end, the Winchester House covered six acres. It contained 160 rooms, 47 fireplaces, 40 staircases, 10,000 windows, 52 skylights, 467 doorways, 6 kitchens, a formal dining room, and a grand ballroom. In all, Sarah spent $5 million constructing her ghost house.

17   Some features of the house are quite odd. For example, it has five heating systems and three elevators. Secret passageways are everywhere, but many lead to blank walls. Several of the staircases don't lead anywhere. One staircase has 40 steps, each only two inches high! One room has nothing but trap doors. Another has a skylight—in the floor. On the second floor, some of the doors open onto thin air.

18   Sarah obsession with the number 13 is evidenced throughout the house. Each light fixture has 13 globes. Some staircases have 13 steps. The house has 13 bathrooms, and Sarah's bathroom has 13 windows.

19   The house occupied Sarah's every waking moment. The work was all she had, for she never invited anyone into the house. Even a president was

turned away from the door. In 1903 President Theodore Roosevelt dropped by for a visit but was informed by a servant that "the house was not open to strangers." He never did gain entrance.

20   But perhaps Sarah wasn't alone in her rambling mansion. In her later years, it was said that every night, when the tower bell tolled midnight, organ music could be heard coming from the house. It couldn't have been Sarah playing, for her fingers had grown so stiff with age that she could hardly hold a pencil.

21   Clearly, Sarah herself believed that the house had ghostly residents, for she dined with them each evening. Servants would set 13 places at the table, heap each plate with food, and fill the crystal goblets with the finest wines. That was Sarah's nightly offering to any spirits who cared to dine. "Good evening," she would say. "I am pleased that you have come to share my food and my house. Please enjoy yourselves." Early each morning, the servants would clear the dining room, although they never revealed whether the food and wine had been touched.

22   Outwardly, Sarah was the perfect hostess, but secretly she was terrified of the ghosts. So that they wouldn't find her when she was sleeping, she slept in a different room every night.

23   Sarah Winchester devoted her life to **making amends** to those who had been killed by Winchester rifles, but the house she labored over wasn't enough to save her. **Despite** Adam Coons's promise that she would not die as long as she kept building, Sarah died there in 1922, at the age of 85. At the time of her death, there was enough material on the site to continue building for another 38 years.

making amends
apologizing

despite
regardless of

24 Because Sarah didn't leave a will, her furnishings were put up for auction. It took six large vans working eight hours a day for six weeks to haul off all her belongings. The following year the house itself was sold. The new owners opened the Winchester House to visitors, charging admission for the opportunity to wander through it. On May 13, 1974, the Winchester House was designated a California Historical Landmark.

25 Today visitors still marvel at the bizarre, sprawling building. Those who visit frequently say that the house is larger today than it was when Sarah died. Since there were no permanent plans for the house, no blueprints, there isn't any way to prove these claims. Still, people insist that new rooms have been added. Could Sarah still be trying to make amends from beyond the grave? Some people think so. Whatever the case, the Winchester House is like no other house on earth—it's an architectural fun house built for the comfort of invisible residents.

Timed Reading

If you have been timed while reading this article, enter your reading time below. Then turn to the Words-per-Minute table on page 129 and look up your reading speed (words per minute). Enter your reading speed on the graph on page 130.

Reading Time: Lesson 2.4

_____ : _____

Minutes   Seconds

COMPREHENSION & CRITICAL THINKING SKILLS

Ⓐ Recognize and Recall Details

Put an **X** in the box next to the answer that correctly completes each statement about the article.

1. Sarah Winchester moved to San Jose, California, from

⬜ **a.** Boston, Massachusetts.

⬜ **b.** San Francisco, California.

⬜ **c.** New Haven, Connecticut.

2. All her life, Sarah had been interested in

⬜ **a.** rifles.

⬜ **b.** the occult.

⬜ **c.** building a great mansion.

3. Sarah went to mediums in order to

⬜ **a.** try to contact her dead husband and baby.

⬜ **b.** ask the spirits of people killed by Winchester rifles how she might make amends to them.

⬜ **c.** find out what she should do with her life.

4. Sarah started adding to her mansion in the

⬜ **a.** early 1900s.

⬜ **b.** 1880s.

⬜ **c.** 1840s.

Ⓑ Find the Main Idea

One statement below expresses the main idea of the article. One statement is too general, or too broad. The other statement explains only part of the article; it is too narrow. Label the statements using the following key:

M Main Idea	**B** Too Broad	**N** Too Narrow

_____ **1.** The house that Sarah Winchester built in Northern California had 47 fireplaces and 40 staircases.

_____ **2.** Sarah Winchester spent most of her life trying to make amends for the deaths of people killed by Winchester rifles.

_____ **3.** Sarah Winchester built a huge, rambling house for the ghosts of the people killed by Winchester rifles.

C Summarize and Paraphrase

1. Look for the important ideas and events in paragraphs 5 and 6. Summarize those paragraphs in several sentences.

_____

_____

_____

_____

2. Put an X in the box next to the best paraphrase of the following sentence from the article:

"In her later years, it was said that every night, when the tower bell tolled midnight, organ music could be heard coming from the house."

☐ **a.** Every night, Sarah played the organ so loudly that her neighbors could hear it.

☐ **b.** After Sarah died, many people said that organ music drifted from the tower at midnight.

☐ **c.** When Sarah was older, people claimed that every night at midnight, the sounds of organ music drifted from the house.

D Make Inferences

When you combine your own experience with information from a text to draw a conclusion that is not directly stated in the text, you are making an inference. The following inferences about the article may or may not be correct. Label the statements using the following key:

C Correct Inference	**F** Faulty Inference

_____ **1.** William Winchester was an evil man.

_____ **2.** Adam Coons, Sarah Winchester's medium, continued to advise her throughout her life.

_____ **3.** If William and Annie had not died, Sarah would never have built her ghost house.

_____ **4.** The materials that were left on the site when Sarah died were used to continue adding to the house.

_____ **5.** Sarah's servants must have known many interesting things about her.

ⓔ Recognize Author's Effect and Intentions

Put an **X** in the box next to the answer.

1. Which of the following statements from the article best describes Sarah Winchester?

   ☐ **a.** In 1862 Sarah Pardee had everything to look forward to.

   ☐ **b.** She'd drive one of her two automobiles—both two-tone lavender and yellow Pierce Arrows.

   ☐ **c.** Sarah had always been intrigued by the occult—the mysteries of the spirit world.

2. The author probably wrote this article in order to

   ☐ **a.** tell the reader about Sarah Winchester and her house.

   ☐ **b.** convey a tragic mood.

   ☐ **c.** express an opinion about the harm done by Winchester rifles.

ⓕ Evaluate and Create

1. Which of the following statements is an opinion rather than a fact? Put an X in the box next to the answer.

   ☐ **a.** Some details of the house are quite odd.

   ☐ **b.** Just one month after her birth, baby Annie died from a mysterious illness.

   ☐ **c.** In 1884 Sarah sold her home in New Haven and traveled to California.

2. Put an X in the box next to the clause that correctly completes the following statement:

   You can predict that if Sarah Winchester had not consulted Adam Coons,

   ☐ **a.** she would have lost interest in the occult.

   ☐ **b.** she would not have moved to California.

   ☐ **c.** her husband's ghost would have spoken directly to her.

3. Choose from the letters below to complete the following statement. Write the letters on the lines.

   On the positive side, _____, but on the negative side, _____.

   a. Sarah attached special importance to the number 13

   b. Sarah remained frightened of the ghosts she believed still haunted her

   c. Sarah created a fascinating house

Krakatoa: The Doomsday Crack Heard 'Round the World

The island and volcano of Krakatoa is in Sunda Strait, Indonesia, situated between Java and Sumatra. Much of the island is covered with lava from the volcano.

Before You Read
Use Prior Knowledge

You already know about many things from your own life experience. Think about what you already know about the topic. As you read, you can build on what you know.

- What do you know about volcanoes?

- What have you read or heard about Indonesia?

1   In August 1883 the people of Texas heard a tremendous boom that they thought was cannon fire. What the Texans actually heard was the sound of a series of volcanic eruptions on Krakatoa, an island halfway around the world in the South Pacific. The sound from Krakatoa (now part of Indonesia) was probably one of the loudest noises in human history.

2   Krakatoa was a small island—only six miles square—between Java and Sumatra. It almost disappeared from the face of the Earth, and the noise of its passing was heard halfway around the world. On Borneo, 350 miles from Krakatoa, the islanders believed the sound was caused by an evil spirit seeking revenge. They were terrified and, in an attempt to escape from the spirit, jumped off a cliff, killing themselves.

3   The tremendous noise was not the volcano's only way of announcing its eruption. A cloud of steam and ash rose to a height greater than 36,000 feet—more than seven miles. A ship more than 15 miles from Krakatoa was covered with volcanic ash to a depth of 15 feet. Ash fell on ships as far away as 1,600 miles from Krakatoa and eventually covered an area of 300,000 square miles.

4   Some of the lava that also spewed from the volcano mixed with air and hardened into a stone called *pumice*. The air in pumice makes it so light that it floats. Pumice from Krakatoa was blown into the sea, where ocean currents spread it over a vast area of the Pacific. For 18 months after the eruption, ships plowed through seas covered with great chunks of floating pumice until the pumice stones absorbed so much water that they lost their **buoyancy** and sank.

buoyancy
tendency to float

5   The volcano's light volcanic ash and dust rose into the atmosphere, where winds carried it all over

the Earth. Weather all over the globe was affected for months after the eruption. For an entire year, only 87 percent of the usual amount of sunlight was able to penetrate the umbrella of dust and reach the Earth. For two years, the reflection of the sun on the ash in the upper atmosphere resulted in spectacular sunsets. Sunsets were blue in South America and green in Panama. The skies over the United States glowed so red that people thought the color was the result of gigantic fires. People turned in fire alarms in Poughkeepsie, New York, and in New Haven, Connecticut.

generated
produced

6   The great shock wave **generated** by the eruption swept completely around the world and kept right on going. It circled the globe once, twice . . . seven times in all.

7   Krakatoa's eruption was accompanied by a great earthquake that jolted the seabed under the waters surrounding the island. The seas around Krakatoa rose to a temperature 60 degrees Fahrenheit above normal, and a *tsunami* (tsoo-NAH-mee), a giant sea wave, rolled toward the island. The tsunami reached

attained
reached

a height of 135 feet and **attained** a speed of 600 miles per hour.

8   It was this great hill of moving water that caused

casualties
deaths

most of the 36,000 **casualties** associated with Krakatoa. The wave spread out in all directions and destroyed more than 300 villages in Southeast Asia. The tsunami picked up a gunboat and dropped it at a point 30 feet above sea level and more than a mile inland. All the gunboat's crew members were killed.

9   Giant tidal waves raced from Krakatoa to all parts of the globe. Their effects were felt as far away as the English Channel, some 13,000 miles distant.

10   Krakatoa itself was torn to pieces. Five cubic miles of rock—as much as in some of the world's tallest mountains—were blown into dust. Three-fourths of the island disappeared into dust and air. Those parts of the island that didn't explode into the air sank into the sea. Parts of the island that had been 1,000 feet above sea level now lay 1,000 feet under the ocean.

11   After the eruption, the small piece of Krakatoa that remained was covered with volcanic dust. There were no grass, shrubs, or trees. A single red spider—the only living thing that survived the eruption—spun its web, a web for which there were no more insects.

12   In 1925 a small peak popped up out of the sea next to Krakatoa. More and more of the peak emerged from the sea until a new island was formed. The South Pacific islanders named the newcomer *Anak Krakatoa*, Child of Krakatoa. In 1928, three years after its birth, Anak Krakatoa had a minor eruption. The island continues to **emerge from** the sea and to grow larger and larger.

emerge from
rise out of

13   What will be the fate of Anak Krakatoa? Will it grow into a full-sized island? Will it have a gigantic volcanic eruption? Only time will tell.

....

If you have been timed while reading this article, enter your reading time below. Then turn to the Words-per-Minute table on page 129 and look up your reading speed (words per minute). Enter your reading speed on the graph on page 130.

Timed Reading

Reading Time: Lesson 2.5

_____ : _____
Minutes   Seconds

Ⓐ Recognize and Recall Details

Put an **X** in the box next to the answer that correctly completes each statement about the article.

1. The tremendous eruptions on Krakatoa could be heard as far away as
   - ☐ **a.** Borneo.
   - ☐ **b.** Texas.
   - ☐ **c.** Java and Sumatra.

2. Volcanic ash from Krakatoa covered a ship to a depth of
   - ☐ **a.** 15 inches.
   - ☐ **b.** 15 feet.
   - ☐ **c.** 15 yards.

3. Pumice stones from Krakatoa
   - ☐ **a.** covered large portions of the Atlantic Ocean.
   - ☐ **b.** sank ships in the Pacific Ocean.
   - ☐ **c.** drifted until they became waterlogged and sank.

4. Most of the casualties were caused by
   - ☐ **a.** a giant wave.
   - ☐ **b.** volcanic ash and dust.
   - ☐ **c.** pumice stones.

5. The skies over the United States turned
   - ☐ **a.** blue.
   - ☐ **b.** red.
   - ☐ **c.** green.

Ⓑ Find the Main Idea

One of the statements below expresses the main idea of the article. One statement is too broad—it is too general. The other statement is too narrow—it explains only part of the article. Label the statements using the following key:

M Main Idea	**B** Too Broad	**N** Too Narrow

_____ **1.** The terrible effects of volcanic eruptions on Krakatoa in 1883 were felt around the world.

_____ **2.** Krakatoa is a dramatic example of the power of volcanoes.

_____ **3.** When Krakatoa erupted, volcanic ash fell on ships as far away as 1,600 miles from the island.

C Summarize and Paraphrase

Put an X in the box next to the answer.

1. Below are summaries of the article. Choose the summary that says all the most important things about the article but in the fewest words.

   ☐ **a.** In 1883 a violent series of volcanic eruptions on the island of Krakatoa produced a noise heard halfway around the world.

   ☐ **b.** In 1883 volcanic eruptions and a tsunami destroyed the island of Krakatoa, resulting in about 36,000 casualties. The eruptions sent shock waves around the world and affected the weather all over the globe.

   ☐ **c.** In 1883 a violent series of volcanic eruptions destroyed the island of Krakatoa. There was also a tsunami, which caused most of the 36,000 casualties associated with Krakatoa. Volcanic ash from the eruptions was spread for miles, resulting in spectacular sunsets in many parts of the world.

2. Choose the sentence with the same meaning as this sentence: "A single red spider—the only living thing that survived the eruption—spun its web, a web for which there were no more insects."

   ☐ **a.** The only survivors of the eruption were insects.

   ☐ **b.** The only living thing to survive the eruption was a spider caught in its own web.

   ☐ **c.** The only living thing to survive the eruption was a spider, but there were no longer any insects for it to catch in its web.

D Make Inferences

When you combine your own experience with information from a text to draw a conclusion that is not directly stated in the text, you are making an inference. The following inferences about the article may or may not be correct. Label the statements using the following key:

C Correct Inference	**F** Faulty Inference

_____ **1.** Each time a shock wave from Krakatoa circled the earth it got stronger.

_____ **2.** People in the United States were scared because the skies turned red.

_____ **3.** If any people were on Krakatoa during the explosion, they lost their lives.

_____ **4.** Before Krakatoa's volcano erupted, no one had ever heard of pumice.

_____ **5.** Krakatoa will definitely erupt again.

E Recognize Author's Effect and Intentions

Put an X in the box next to the answer.

1. The author uses the first sentence of the article to
   - ☐ **a.** inform the reader about Texas in 1883.
   - ☐ **b.** describe a noise heard in Texas in 1883.
   - ☐ **c.** emphasize the similarities between the sound of cannon fire and a volcanic eruption.

2. What is the author's purpose in giving the article the title "Krakatoa: The Doomsday Crack Heard 'Round the World"?
   - ☐ **a.** to tell the reader about the volcanic eruptions that destroyed Krakatoa
   - ☐ **b.** to inform the reader about tsunamis
   - ☐ **c.** to describe the sound made by the volcanic eruptions on Krakatoa

3. What does the author imply by saying "For an entire year, the umbrella of dust permitted only 87 percent of the usual amount of sunlight to reach the Earth"?
   - ☐ **a.** For a year, the Earth was brighter and warmer than usual.
   - ☐ **b.** For a year, the Earth was darker and cooler than usual.
   - ☐ **c.** For a year, the sun didn't shine at all on the Earth.

F Evaluate and Create

Put an X in the box next to the answer.

1. Which of the following sentences expresses a fact?
   - ☐ **a.** The sound made by the eruptions on Krakatoa was horrifying.
   - ☐ **b.** For two years after the eruptions, sunsets were green in Panama.
   - ☐ **c.** The eruptions on Krakatoa made the planet more beautiful.

2. From the information in paragraph 11, you can predict that
   - ☐ **a.** the spider would die soon because it had nothing to eat.
   - ☐ **b.** birds would soon eat the spider.
   - ☐ **c.** insects would soon be attracted to the spider's web.

3. How is the series of volcanic eruptions on Krakatoa an example of a disaster?
   - ☐ **a.** The eruptions caused the loudest noise ever known.
   - ☐ **b.** The eruptions caused unusual sunsets around the world.
   - ☐ **c.** The eruptions caused the deaths of at least 36,000 people and destroyed a large part of the island.

The Mokele-Mbembe: Are All the Dinosaurs Gone?

Most people think that dinosaurs died out a long time ago. In recent years, however, people in equatorial Africa have reported seeing a strange creature that looks like a small brontosaurus. They call it Mokele-Mbembe, which means "monstrous animal."

Sometimes a key word, such as *vanished* in paragraph 1, will be unfamiliar to you. There are several things you can do that will help you to clarify the meaning of an unfamiliar word:

- Look for familiar words in the same paragraph. Words you know help you figure out the meaning of unfamiliar words.

- Continue reading. Is there more information ahead that will help you clarify the meaning of the unfamiliar word?

The Mokele-Mbembe: Are All the Dinosaurs Gone?

cataclysmic
disastrous

1   The last of the dinosaurs vanished approximately 65 million years ago. They were wiped out in some **cataclysmic** event. Everyone agrees about that, right? Well, it turns out that not everyone is convinced that *all* the dinosaurs disappeared. For several years, the native people of equatorial Africa have reported seeing some sort of bizarre creature that looks very much like a small version of a brontosaurus.

adapt
adjust

wrought
brought about

2   Is it possible that dinosaurs still roam the Earth in a remote region of the world? Could they have found ways to **adapt** to the arrival of new competitors in the food chain? If so, tropical Africa is the most likely location for them to reside because it's one of the few places on Earth that completely escaped the changes **wrought** by the great ice ages. For that reason, tropical Africa today remains extremely similar to the way it looked 65 million years ago.

3   Certain areas of equatorial Africa have only been explored during the past 150 years or so. Could the explorers have missed something? By now, of course, almost every mile of Africa has been examined, and the odds of any strange or unidentified creature surviving undetected grow slimmer.

4   Still, in the remote regions of what are now the Democratic Republic of the Congo and Gabon, reports persist of a dinosaur-like monster. These reports, some of which appear in old European books and journals, go back at least 200 years. In 1913, for instance, a German explorer named Freiherr Von Stein summarized several sightings of a beast that the pygmies call *Mokele-Mbembe*, which means "monstrous animal." The explorer wrote:

> The animal is said to be a brownish-grey color with smooth skin, its size approximately that of an elephant… It is said to have a very long and **flexible** neck and only one tooth, but a very long one. A few spoke about a long muscular tail like that of an alligator. Canoes coming near it are said to be doomed; the animal kills the crews but without eating the bodies.

flexible
elastic

5   In 1979 an expedition, led by zoologist James Powell, set out to look for Mokele-Mbembe. Like a police officer looking for a criminal suspect, Powell showed local people images of a sauropod, a herbivorous, or plant-eating, dinosaur that is similar to a brontosaurus. Several villagers recognized the creature, which they called N'yamala, and said that it lived in the deep swamps of Gabon. They added that it had blood-red eyes, a huge mouth, and one tooth.

6   A local witch doctor also claimed to have seen the creature, and he described it as being mostly neck and tail, more than 30 feet long, and at least as heavy as an elephant. After studying the record, Powell concluded that N'yamala was the same creature as Mokele-Mbembe. Although he reported many sightings by native peoples, Powell never saw the beast for himself.

7   In 1981 an American named Herman Regusters went searching for Mokele-Mbembe. He reached Lake

Tele where most of the sightings occurred. Quite possibly, Regusters was the first outsider to see this small round lake in the Republic of the Congo. He also became the first westerner to claim he saw the monster. He gathered sound recordings, plaster cast footprints, and samples of droppings. Regusters even took photographs of the beast, but the prints turned out foggy and unclear.

8   The next expedition, in 1983, was led by Marcellin Agnagna, a zoologist from the Republic of the Congo's Brazzaville Zoo. He, too, reported seeing Mokele-Mbembe at Lake Tele. Agnagna claimed that the animal was in the lake about 300 yards from shore. He described the creature as a reptile about 16 feet long with a thin reddish head, oval eyes like a crocodile, a long neck, and a broad black back.

9   Since then there have been at least three other expeditions to find Mokele-Mbembe; however, none of these has resulted in more sightings of the creature. One Japanese group claimed that the animal probably doesn't reside in Lake Tele. Instead, they say, Mokele-Mbembe lives in the *molibos*, the small jungle streams that flow into the lake.

10   There are skeptics, however, that aren't convinced Mokele-Mbembe exists. In his 1997 book *No Mercy*, travel writer Redmond O'Hanlon details his search with Macellin Agnagna to find the mysterious African dinosaur. Agnagna's grandfather gave both men good luck charms to protect them from evil spirits at Lake Tele. O'Hanlon believed he would need these talismans because another native man predicted that he would die a "long, messy, **mutilated** death" at Lake Tele.

mutilated
disfigured

11   O'Hanlon did not die, but he did become very sick. During his illness he had wild, bizarre dreams.

When at last he emerged from the jungle, he was weak, filthy, and totally exhausted. As for the Mokele-Mbembe, O'Hanlon was convinced that the eyewitnesses had seen nothing more than forest elephants crossing the lake with their trunks raised. Another possible explanation is that the "dinosaur" is actually a python. Pythons are not true water snakes; they swim with their heads above the water's surface. As they swim, their long bodies trail behind them making bumps in the water.

12   Perhaps, though, O'Hanlon and the other skeptics are incorrect. Perhaps the Mokele-Mbembe is just too elusive to be captured, and the Age of the Dinosaurs isn't really over after all.

If you have been timed while reading this article, enter your reading time below. Then turn to the Words-per-Minute table on page 129 and look up your reading speed (words per minute). Enter your reading speed on the graph on page 130.

Timed Reading

Reading Time: Lesson 3.1

_____ : _____

Minutes   Seconds

COMPREHENSION & CRITICAL THINKING SKILLS

A Recognize and Recall Details

Put an **X** in the box next to the answer that correctly completes each statement about the article.

1. The pygmy term *Mokele-Mbembe* means
   - ☐ **a.** "brontosaurus."
   - ☐ **b.** "dinosaur."
   - ☐ **c.** "monstrous animal."

2. The German explorer who wrote about the beast in 1913 was
   - ☐ **a.** Freiherr Von Stein.
   - ☐ **b.** James Powell.
   - ☐ **c.** Marcellin Agnagna

3. Both Regusters and Agnagna saw Mokole-Mbembe
   - ☐ **a.** in Gabon.
   - ☐ **b.** in Brazzaville.
   - ☐ **c.** at Lake Tele.

4. During Redmond O'Hanlon's search to find the African dinosaur, he
   - ☐ **a.** became very sick.
   - ☐ **b.** died a long, messy death.
   - ☐ **c.** took pictures of the Mokele-Mbembe.

5. O'Hanlon believes that people claiming to have seen the Mokele-Mbembe actually saw
   - ☐ **a.** a python.
   - ☐ **b.** an elephant.
   - ☐ **c.** an alligator.

B Find the Main Idea

One of the statements below expresses the main idea of the article. One statement is too broad. The other statement is too narrow—it explains only part of the article. Label the statements using the following key:

M Main Idea	**B** Too Broad	**N** Too Narrow

_____ 1. A dinosaur known as Mokele-Mbembe is said to live in remote regions of equatorial Africa. None of the explorers who have looked for it have ever proven its existence, however.

_____ 2. American explorer Herman Regusters said he saw Mokele-Mbembe after he reached Lake Tele.

_____ 3. Tropical Africa is the most likely place for a living dinosaur to be found today because the region escaped the changes brought about by the great ice ages.

C Summarize and Paraphrase

1. Complete the following summary of the article using the lettered phrases from the phrase bank below. Write the letters on the lines.

> **Phrase Bank**
>
> **a.** early reports of the monster in Africa
>
> **b.** theories about what the "dinosaur" really is
>
> **c.** recent expeditions undertaken to search for the beast

After an introduction, the article about the Mokele-Mbembe discusses _____, goes on to explain _____, and ends with _____.

2. Choose the sentence with the same meaning as this sentence: "As for the Mokele-Mbembe, O'Hanlon was convinced that the eyewitnesses had seen nothing more than forest elephants crossing the lake with their trunks raised."

   ☐ **a.** O'Hanlon mistook elephants crossing the lake with raised trunks for the Mokele-Mbembe.

   ☐ **b.** O'Hanlon thought that those claiming to have seen the Mokele-Mbembe in the lake had actually seen elephants with raised trunks.

   ☐ **c.** The eyewitnesses told O'Hanlon that they had seen elephants with raised trunks and not the Mokele-Mbembe.

D Make Inferences

When you combine your own experience with information from a text to draw a conclusion that is not directly stated in the text, you are making an inference. The following inferences about the article may or may not be correct. Label the statements using the following key:

> **C** Correct Inference   **F** Faulty Inference

_____ **1.** Dinosaurs could not still be alive in North America.

_____ **2.** The Mokele-Mbembe hunts and kills people for food.

_____ **3.** Many villagers in equatorial Africa believe that the legend of the Mokele-Mbembe is true.

_____ **4.** The Mokele-Mbembe cannot swim.

_____ **5.** Freiherr Von Stein saw the mysterious African dinosaur.

E Recognize Author's Effect and Intentions

Put an X in the box next to the answer.

1. What is the author's purpose in writing the article?

   ☐ **a.** to tell the reader about the attempts to find a dinosaur-like monster reportedly seen in equatorial Africa

   ☐ **b.** to describe equatorial Africa

   ☐ **c.** to emphasize the similarities between dinosaurs and elephants

2. What is the author's purpose for writing paragraph 7?

   ☐ **a.** to describe Lake Tele in the Democratic Republic of the Congo

   ☐ **b.** to compare the Mokele-Mbembe's footprints with those of other animals

   ☐ **c.** to inform readers about Herman Reguster's efforts to find the Mokele-Mbembe

F Evaluate and Create

Put an X in the box next to the answer.

1. Which of the following statements is an opinion rather than a fact?

   ☐ **a.** "Perhaps the Mokele-Mbembe is just too elusive to be caught, and the Age of the Dinosaurs isn't really over after all."

   ☐ **b.** "Tropical Africa looks pretty much as it did 65 million years ago."

   ☐ **c.** "Pythons are not true water snakes; they swim with their head above the water's surface."

2. From what the article told about Marcellin Agnagna's first expedition, you can predict that he would

   ☐ **a.** not agree with O'Hanlon's theory about the Mokele-Mbembe.

   ☐ **b.** agree with O'Hanlon's theory about the Mokele-Mbembe.

   ☐ **c.** throw away his good luck charm after completing his expedition with O'Hanlon.

3. Choose from the letters below to correctly complete the following statement. Write the letters on the lines.

   In the article, _____ and _____ are most alike.

   ☐ **a.** the monster known as the Mokele-Mbembe

   ☐ **b.** the monster known as the N'yamala

   ☐ **c.** the monster known as the python

Spiritualism: Fact or Fraud

Members of the spiritualism movement of the nineteenth century claimed that some people could move objects with their minds.

Read the title and the first sentence of the article. Connect what you will be reading to things you have learned or experienced.

- Do you think it is possible to communicate with the spirits of dead people? Why or why not?

- Describe people you have heard about who claim to communicate with spirits. Do you believe them?

Spiritualism: Fact or Fraud

1   Spiritualism—the belief that a person's spirit survives after death and can communicate with the living through a medium—got its start on Friday, March 31, 1848. On that day two young women, Margaret and Katherine Fox, reported having the first of a number of "spirit conversations." Those conversations were to make the Fox family, and spiritualism, the talk of the country.

2   In December 1847 the Fox family moved into a house in the small town of Hydesville, in upstate New York. Within two months, strange rapping sounds began to be heard at all hours—but only when the two daughters were present. Margaret and Katherine—or Kate, as she was called—weren't at all disturbed by the noises.

3   Their parents, on the other hand, were distressed, especially their mother, who was a devout Methodist. She was convinced that the strange rapping was the work of the devil. Hearing that, Margaret and Kate laughingly named the phenomenon "Mr. Splitfoot," because the devil is frequently depicted as having **cloven** hooves.

cloven
divided into two parts

4   Mrs. Fox tried unsuccessfully to locate the source of the rappings. Then, on March 31, after the family

had retired for the evening, the rapping sounds began anew and were so persistent that no one could remain asleep. Finally, one of the girls sat up and called out, "Here, Mr. Splitfoot, do as I do." She snapped her fingers once and was answered with a single rap. She then snapped her fingers several more times and was answered with an equal number of raps.

5   By that time the girls' parents had joined them, and together they worked out a simple code. Phrasing questions that could be answered yes or no, or with a number, Mrs. Fox interrogated the knocking intruder. The spirit answered all her questions correctly.

6   The Foxes were informed that Mr. Splitfoot was the spirit of a man who in life had been a peddler. He had supposedly been robbed of $500, murdered in that very house, and buried in the cellar.

7   The following morning the Foxes tried to verify the story. Town records contained no mention of any peddlers being murdered, nor did a search of the cellar yield any bones. What did happen, however, was that news of the rapping sounds and "conversation" became known throughout the town. Before long the Fox's house was crowded with curious visitors from all over the Northeast.

8   The excitement around the Fox house became so great that Mrs. Fox sent Margaret and Kate to live with their older sister, Leah, in Rochester. Mrs. Fox hoped that the spirit would not follow the girls, but it did.

9   Since Rochester was a large city, once the news of Mr. Splitfoot got out, even greater crowds converged on the Fox sisters. Soon all three sisters were the center of a devoted "spirit circle," which held nightly meetings in Leah's house.

10   Soon the shrewd Leah, who was more than 20 years older than her sisters, conceived the idea of making money from the phenomenon. She organized a public demonstration in Corinthian Hall, Rochester's largest auditorium, and charged a fee of one dollar for admission, a tidy sum in those days.

11   The "rapping telegraph," as the question-and-answer system was dubbed, was a rousing success. Two more exhibitions were held, both before capacity crowds. Not everyone was taken with the show, however. Some people were determined to prove that the Fox sisters were frauds.

12   Committees were formed to investigate the performances, but nothing dishonest was discovered. Still, enraged doubters began throwing firecrackers onto the stage and threatening the sisters. The police hustled the women to safety.

13   The sisters began touring and also offered private demonstrations. They attracted large crowds wherever they performed, and their clients for the private sessions included the rich and the famous. Among them was Mary Todd Lincoln, who wished to communicate with her recently assassinated husband, President Abraham Lincoln.

discredit
cast doubt on

14   As spiritualism spread, arguments for and against it continued to rage. The believers far outnumbered the nonbelievers. Indeed, the harder the skeptics tried to **discredit** the Fox sisters, the more firmly their supporters believed.

15   Then, on October 21, 1888—40 years after the initial incident at Hydesville—Margaret Fox gave a special demonstration at the Academy of Music in New York City for the purpose of confessing to defrauding the public. A newspaper account of the day describes the reaction of the audience to the news:

There was a dead silence; everybody in the hall knew they were looking upon the woman who was principally responsible for spiritualism. She stood upon a little pine table, with nothing on her feet but stockings. As she remained motionless, loud distinct rappings were heard, now in the flies (above the stage), now behind the scenes, now in the gallery.

16   Margaret was making the rapping sounds by snapping a joint in her big toe. The acoustical properties of the hall gave the illusion that the sounds were coming from various locations.

17   You might think that this astonishing **revelation** spelled the end of spiritualism, but it didn't. People refused to believe Margaret, or they argued that she had been forced into a false confession—by the churches, perhaps, or by the newspapers. Even if the Fox sisters were frauds, some people argued, that didn't mean that all spiritualists were frauds.

revelation
discovery

18   Two years later, the sisters retracted the confession and resumed their demonstrations. Both Margaret and Kate, however, were deep in the grip of alcoholism and died soon after. Only the **wily** Leah was able to go on, and she did, amassing a small fortune.

wily
shrewd

19   Given the story of the Fox sisters, you might reasonably conclude that spiritualism was a hoax. Before you make up your mind, however, consider the story of Leonora Piper.

20   In 1884 Leonora Piper, plagued by a series of ailments, sought relief from a psychic healer in Boston. Though her first visit offered no relief, Leonora later said that some powerful force commanded her to visit the healer a second time. She did, and that time she felt herself drawn into a trance. Furniture whirled about her, her mind reeled, and she began to speak,

but not in her own voice. It was the voice of a dead girl named Chlorine.

21 Soon Leonora was capable of entering into a trance at will. Over the next four years she was possessed by a number of spirits, each, it seemed, trying to gain control over her. They included the spirits of some famous people, such as actress Sarah Siddons, poet Henry Wadsworth Longfellow, and composer Johann Sebastian Bach.

22 Leonora became the subject of a serious study. William James of Harvard College and Richard Hodgson of the American Society for Psychical Research "adopted" her. From 1887 until 1911, several people interested in spiritualism studied Leonora, detectives trailed her, and people copied down her every word. Every facet of her life was scrutinized for fraud, but none was ever found.

dominate
control

23 During that time one spirit began to **dominate** Leonora in her trances. The spirit spoke English with a heavy French accent and called itself Dr. Phinuit.

24 In one of their many tests, James and Hodgson assembled a group of people and introduced each of them to Leonora under false names. When Leonora dropped into a trance, Dr. Phinuit took over and revealed details about the people that Leonora could not possibly have known, including places, dates, and even their actual names. Every attempt to throw her off the track failed. The same test was conducted in England by members of the British Society for Psychical Research, with the same results.

25 Oliver Lodge, head of the British committee, devised one final test he believed would be foolproof. Lodge, it seems, had twin uncles, Robert and Jerry. Jerry had died 20 years earlier. At a séance, Lodge

showed Dr. Phinuit a gold watch. The doctor spoke at once, "It belonged to your uncle," he said. "Your uncle Jerry." Then followed a rambling conversation between Lodge and Dr. Phinuit, during which the doctor revealed an astonishing number of anecdotes about Lodge's dead Uncle Jerry. Lodge was convinced that Leonora was an extraordinary medium.

26   At the conclusion of the séances, Oliver Lodge and his fellow committee members wrote a detailed report to the British society. They concluded that they had never before encountered anyone like Leonora Piper. They were in awe of her powers.

27   As for Dr. Phinuit, however, the report stated that he was never a real person. The story of his life was contradictory, and his medical knowledge was weak. Phinuit, the report suggested, was a variant of the name used by the Boston psychic whom Leonora first visited. Dr. Phinuit, they concluded, was Leonora's *alter ego*—another side of her personality that she got in touch with only when she entered a trance. She gave him his name unconsciously; there was no attempt at fraud. Her contact with spirits, the British group believed, was genuine.

....

If you have been timed while reading this article, enter your reading time below. Then turn to the Words-per-Minute table on page 129 and look up your reading speed (words per minute). Enter your reading speed on the graph on page 130.

Timed Reading

Reading Time: Lesson 3.2

_____ : _____

Minutes   Seconds

Ⓐ Recognize and Recall Details

Put an **X** in the box next to the answer that correctly completes each statement about the article.

1. The Fox sisters lived in
   - ☐ **a.** England.
   - ☐ **b.** New York.
   - ☐ **c.** the Midwest.

2. According to Margaret Fox, the rappings were made by
   - ☐ **a.** Dr. Phinuit.
   - ☐ **b.** snapping her fingers.
   - ☐ **c.** cracking her toe.

3. When Margaret Fox admitted to fraud,
   - ☐ **a.** the belief in spiritualism continued anyway.
   - ☐ **b.** she and her sisters were put in jail.
   - ☐ **c.** the spiritualism movement ended.

4. The spiritualism movement was strong during the
   - ☐ **a.** first half of the nineteenth century.
   - ☐ **b.** last half of the nineteenth century.
   - ☐ **c.** early twentieth century.

5. When in a trance, Leonora Piper could
   - ☐ **a.** speak foreign languages.
   - ☐ **b.** compose music.
   - ☐ **c.** identify strangers.

Ⓑ Find the Main Idea

One of the statements below expresses the main idea of the article. One statement is too broad. The other statement is too narrow—it explains only part of the article. Label the statements using the following key:

M Main Idea	**B** Too Broad	**N** Too Narrow

____ **1.** The Fox sisters toured the country, claiming that they were able to contact the dead.

____ **2.** The spiritualism movement, which claimed that spirits can contact the living through a sensitive human being, included both frauds and seemingly true mediums.

____ **3.** The spiritualism movement raised many interesting questions about supernatural issues.

C Summarize and Paraphrase

1. Complete the following one-sentence summary of the article using the lettered phrases from the phrase bank below. Write the letters on the lines.

> **Phrase Bank**
>
> **a.** the Fox sisters' "contact" with Mr. Splitfoot
>
> **b.** Leonora Piper's experience with spirits
>
> **c.** the Fox sisters' performances and eventual confession

The article about spiritualism begins with _____, goes on to explain _____, and ends with _____.

2. Choose the sentence with the same meaning as this sentence: "Though her first visit offered no relief, Leonora later said that some powerful force commanded her to visit the healer a second time."

☐ **a.** Even though the first visit had done no good, the healer ordered Leonora to visit him a second time.

☐ **b.** Even though her first visit had done no good, Leonora felt that a force within her demanded that she return to the healer.

☐ **c.** Even though her first visit had done no good, Leonora decided on her own that she would visit the healer a second time.

D Make Inferences

When you combine your own experience with information from a text to draw a conclusion that is not directly stated in the text, you are making an inference. The following inferences about the article may or may not be correct. Label the statements using the following key:

> **C** Correct Inference   **F** Faulty Inference

____ **1.** Leonora Piper is the only medium ever found to be honest.

____ **2.** The Fox sisters all felt guilty for the fraud they engaged in.

____ **3.** In the beginning, Margaret secretly told her two sisters about the trick of cracking her toe.

____ **4.** The psychic researchers forced Leonora to subject herself to their tests.

____ **5.** Many people are fascinated with the subject of spirits.

E ⬤ Recognize Author's Effect and Intentions

Put an X in the box next to the answer.

1. The author uses the first sentence of the article to

   ☐ **a.** tell the reader when spiritualism began.

   ☐ **b.** entertain the reader with a story about spiritualism.

   ☐ **c.** compare the living world to the spirit world.

2. In this article, "Not everyone was taken with the show, however" means that

   ☐ **a.** some people weren't able to go to see the show.

   ☐ **b.** not everyone was impressed by the show.

   ☐ **c.** many people went to the show alone.

3. The author probably wrote this article in order to

   ☐ **a.** express his or her distaste for spiritualism.

   ☐ **b.** persuade the reader to consult a medium.

   ☐ **c.** acquaint the reader with both sides of a controversial issue.

F ⬤ Evaluate and Create

Put an X in the box next to the answer.

1. Choose the statement below that expresses an opinion.

   ☐ **a.** The Fox sisters admitted to being frauds.

   ☐ **b.** The British Society for Psychical Research wrote a detailed report about Leonora Piper.

   ☐ **c.** No one with any intelligence believes in spiritualism.

2. From the article, you can predict that if Leonora Piper had given public demonstrations of her trances,

   ☐ **a.** many people would have come to see her.

   ☐ **b.** no one would have come to see her.

   ☐ **c.** the Fox sisters would have accused her of being a fraud.

3. What was a major cause of excitement in the Fox house?

   ☐ **a.** the discovery that Mr. Splitfoot was the spirit of a murdered peddler

   ☐ **b.** Margaret and Kate's visit to their sister Leah's home

   ☐ **c.** the fact that news of the rappings spread throughout the Northeast

Chupacabra: Bloodthirsty Beast

The legend of the Chupacabra, or goatsucker, is based on eyewitness descriptions. The Chupacabra was first reported in Puerto Rico in the mid-1990s.

When you don't know much about a topic, you can get more information about it before you read. You can:

- ask classmates whether they know the legend of Chupacabra, and if so, how they learned about it.

- ask classmates to share what they know about other legends.

Chupacabra: Bloodthirsty Beast

1   The panic began in 1995 in Puerto Rico, when farmers began finding the bloodless corpses of goats, chickens, rabbits, dogs, sheep, pigs, and other animals. The victims had all had their blood drained through puncture wounds, usually in the neck or chest. The killings soon reached **epidemic** proportions in the hills of Puerto Rico. Was this the work of wild animals or was it the work of some supernatural beast with a vampire's thirst for blood?

epidemic
widespread

2   To many people, the answer was obvious— the grim massacre was the handiwork of a strange monster described as part bat, part kangaroo, part insect, and a little bit of reptile and armadillo tossed in for good measure. People who have seen the creature report that despite being only three to four feet tall it is still a terrifying sight. It has fangs, a row of spikes running down its back, bat wings, kangaroo legs, and bulging red eyes that look like burning coal. In Puerto Rico and other Spanish-speaking places, the beast has been given a name that reminds everyone of its love for goat's blood. It is called *Chupacabra*, which is Spanish for "goatsucker."

3   Whoever or whatever the Chupacabra is, it must have some relatives, because it seems to have been in several places at one time. Chupacabras have been sighted in San Francisco, Miami, San Antonio, New

York City, and even London and Moscow. Witnesses have also reported seeing them in Costa Rica, Peru, and Ecuador. But the gruesome little creatures have done their worst mischief in Puerto Rico and Mexico.

4   In Mexico the monster has caused genuine fear and panic. In 1996 the *Los Angeles Times* ran a story about the creature. The headline read: "Tales of a Bloodthirsty Beast Terrify Mexico." A *Reuters* headline put it this way: "Mysterious Vampire Beast Spreads Panic in Mexico." The *Tucson Weekly* did a cover story on Chupacabras titled "Hellmonkeys from Beyond."

5   Where do the Chupacabras come from? Some people believe they must have come down to Earth from outer space. Others insist they are **mutants**—the results of an experiment gone wrong. People swear that wherever this **demon** came from, it is not a creature one might find in the wild or in a zoo.

mutants
creatures that have been drastically changed

demon
evil spirit

6   While skeptics laugh off the Chupacabra, many other people are nearly scared to death. Take the case of Naucalpan, a small village in the Mexican state of Sinaloa. There a local farmer saw a batlike creature swoop down on his corral and kill 24 of his sheep. All the dead animals had puncture marks on their necks, and their blood had been sucked until their bodies were as dry as a bone.

7   A major Mexican TV network rushed a camera crew to Naucalpan, and it broadcast news of the attack across Mexico. "This created a great panic," said Desiderio Aguilar, a Sinaloa police official. Many people were convinced that Chupacabra was responsible for the deaths. "Mothers have quit sending their children to school for fear they could be attacked on the way," said Aguilar. "Farmers who used to start work at 4 A.M. to beat the heat aren't leaving their homes until well after daybreak."

In some places, farmers armed with torches attacked bats in their caves, hoping to burn out any Chupacabras who might be hiding there.

8   More reports of attacks and killings flooded in from other parts of Mexico. In the town of Villalba, 20 roosting chickens were found dead with holes in their chests. Victor Santiago, the chief of police, was **stunned**. He said, "We have no explanation because it is difficult for any killer to catch a chicken that's asleep in a tree. It's a very strange case. A very complicated case."

stunned
shocked

9   In a few instances, a Chupacabra is reported to have attacked humans. A 21-year-old woman claimed that one of these beasts bit off her ear. In another widely reported case, a Chupacabra supposedly hopped through a young boy's open bedroom window and landed on him, smelling "like a wet dog." Although the boy wasn't injured, his aunt was called in to give her opinion of the event. Without hesitation, she said that the footprints on the little boy's chest were made by a Chupacabra. Angel Pulido, a Mexican farmer, called in reporters to show them bite marks on his right arm, which he claimed he got from "a giant bat that resembled a witch."

10   There was also a Chupacabra panic in Puerto Rico. In the small town of Canovanas, 30 people reported seeing a bizarre creature swoop out of the sky and leap over trees. Meanwhile, animals kept turning up dead with puncture wounds in their necks and chests. Ismael Aguayo was a police detective who checked out the reports. He said, "We are all very worried here. Our animals are dying at an alarming rate… But we are worried that our children will be next."

11   Not everyone in Mexico or Puerto Rico thinks that the **ghoulish** killings were done by Chupacabras. Most investigators blamed the attacks on wild dogs or

ghoulish
creepy

cougars. In Mexico, to calm fears, federal experts conducted autopsies in Sinaloa on dead sheep. They concluded that the attacks had been made by coyotes or other natural predators.

12   These experts also set traps to prove that wild predators, not the supernatural Chupacabras, were killing the animals. They placed live sheep in the same corral where the initial killings had taken place. All-night guards observed the corral. "Late at night, a few wild dogs showed up and attacked the sheep—leaving the same marks found on the first dead sheep," said Desiderio Aguilar. The investigators then captured the dogs and showed them to the townspeople.

13   Still, even this evidence can't stop the public's fear of Chupacabras. Too many people have seen too much to be convinced that the Chupacabras are not a real danger. Hector Armstrong, a Princeton University student who started his own Web page on Chupacabras, thinks outsiders shouldn't dismiss those eyewitness accounts. "While it's funny to laugh about Chupacabras," he said, "we should not discount the mounds of evidence people have found, nor should we disrespect the reports of hundreds of people."

....

If you have been timed while reading this article, enter your reading time below. Then turn to the Words-per-Minute table on page 129 and look up your reading speed (words per minute). Enter your reading speed on the graph on page 130.

Timed Reading

Reading Time: Lesson 3.3

_____ : _____

Minutes   Seconds

Ⓐ Recognize and Recall Details

Put an X in the box next to the answer that completes each statement.

1. *Chupacabra* is Spanish for

☐ **a.** "goatsucker."

☐ **b.** "bloodsucker."

☐ **c.** "hellmonkey."

2. Some eyewitnesses think that Chupacabras came from

☐ **a.** London.

☐ **b.** a zoo.

☐ **c.** outer space.

3. All of the dead animals in Naucalpan

☐ **a.** had footprints on their chests.

☐ **b.** had their ears bitten off.

☐ **c.** had puncture marks on their necks.

4. After a Chupacabra attack in Canovanas, many people feared that

☐ **a.** Ismael Aguayo might be attacked next.

☐ **b.** their children might be attacked next.

☐ **c.** others might not believe their stories.

Ⓑ Find the Main Idea

**One of the statements below expresses the main idea of the article.
One statement is too broad. The other statement is too narrow—it explains
only part of the article. Label the statements using the following key:**

M Main Idea	**B** Too Broad	**N** Too Narrow

____ **1.** A farmer in Naucalpan saw a strange creature swoop down on his corral and kill 24 of his sheep.

____ **2.** People who claim to have seen the Chupacabra say that it is not a normal creature.

____ **3.** In countries such as Puerto Rico and Mexico, people have reported seeing a strange batlike creature that drains the blood from its animal victims.

C Summarize and Paraphrase

Put an X in the box next to the answer.

1. Below are summaries of the article. Choose the summary that says all the most important things about the article but in the fewest words.

   ☐ **a.** Chupacabras have attacked and killed many animals. These creatures make puncture wounds in their victims' neck or chest and drain out all the blood.

   ☐ **b.** Chupacabras have reportedly attacked and drained the blood from many animals in Puerto Rico and Mexico. Although evidence has suggested that Chupacabras are actually wild dogs or other natural predators, many people remain unconvinced.

   ☐ **c.** Bloodthirsty Chupacabra attacks have been reported in many parts of the world, but most have occurred in Puerto Rico and Mexico. Chupacabras, which eyewitnesses have described as part bat and part kangaroo, reportedly drain the blood from their animal victims. There have also been a few instances of Chupacabra attacks on humans.

2. Choose the sentence that correctly restates the following sentence from the article: "A Chupacabra supposedly hopped through a young boy's open bedroom window and landed on him, smelling 'like a wet dog.'"

   ☐ **a.** A Chupacabra jumped on a boy who smelled like a wet dog.

   ☐ **b.** A boy thought that a Chupacabra jumped into his room, but it turned out to be a wet dog.

   ☐ **c.** A Chupacabra that jumped into a boy's bedroom smelled to him like a wet dog.

D Make Inferences

The following inferences about the article may or may not be correct. Label the statements using the following key:

> **C** Correct Inference   **F** Faulty Inference

____ **1.** Chupacabras are like bloodsucking vampires.

____ **2.** Chupacabras kill more goats than mountain lions.

____ **3.** Many farmers would kill Chupacabras if they could.

____ **4.** Everyone will soon stop believing in Chupacabras.

E Recognize Author's Effect and Intentions

Put an X in the box next to the answer.

1. The author uses the first sentence of the article to

☐ **a.** inform the reader that something caused a panic in Puerto Rico in 1995.

☐ **b.** describe Puerto Rico.

☐ **c.** persuade the reader to visit Puerto Rico.

2. What does the author mean by the statement "People swear that wherever this demon came from, it is not a creature one might find in the wild or in a zoo"?

☐ **a.** Most people thought that the Chupacabra was much too wild ever to live in a zoo.

☐ **b.** Most people wanted to put the Chupacabra in the zoo.

☐ **c.** The Chupacabra did not look at all like any animal that had ever been seen before.

3. The author probably wrote this article in order to

☐ **a.** express an opinion about Chupacabras.

☐ **b.** inform the reader about Chupacabras.

☐ **c.** convince the reader that Chupacabras do not exist.

F Evaluate and Create

Put an X in the box next to the answer.

1. Which of the following statements is an opinion rather than a fact?

☐ **a.** "The *Tucson Weekly* did a cover story on Chupacabras."

☐ **b.** "In Mexico, to calm fears, federal experts conducted autopsies in Sinaloa on dead sheep."

☐ **c.** "We should not discount the mounds of evidence people have found."

2. From what Victor Santiago says in paragraph 8, you can predict that he would claim that

☐ **a.** natural predators killed the chickens in Villalba.

☐ **b.** a Chupacabra killed the chickens in Villalba.

☐ **c.** farmers killed the chickens in Villalba.

Challenger:
The Final Countdown

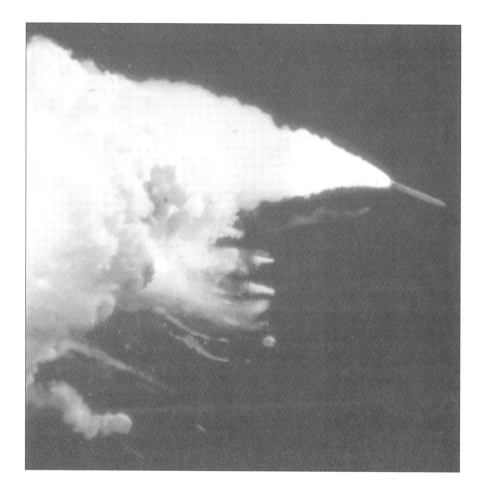

On January 28, 1986, the spacecraft Challenger exploded one minute and 15 seconds after liftoff from Cape Canaveral, Florida. Fragments could be seen against a background of fire and smoke. The tragedy shocked millions of people and left the nation in mourning.

To preview the lesson:

- look at the photograph.

- read the title of the article and the photo caption.

- skim the article to get some idea of the way it is organized.

- read the questions after the article. As you read the article,
  look for information that will help you answer the questions.

Challenger:
The Final Countdown

1   What happened to Christa McAuliffe, Francis
Scobee, Ellison Onizuka, Judith Resnick, Michael
Smith, Ronald McNair, and Gregory Jarvis, the crew
members of the space shuttle *Challenger*, on January
28, 1986, shocked millions of people and left a nation
in mourning.

2   For Christa McAuliffe, the journey began in 1984
when President Ronald Reagan announced that a
teacher would be the first civilian to travel in space.
McAuliffe, a social studies teacher from New
Hampshire, eagerly applied for the opportunity.
She was among 11,000 teachers who submitted
applications to the National Aeronautics and Space
Administration (NASA). Ever since childhood,
McAuliffe had been fascinated with space. She told
NASA how excited she was when she watched the
first satellites being launched and when Alan Shepard
became the first American in space in 1961. She
explained that she was always envious of astronauts
and hoped that eventually women would have
careers in space, too.

3   NASA selected McAuliffe for the teacher-in-space
program in 1985. As part of her historic mission, she
planned to keep journals detailing her experience as

a "pioneer" space traveler, and to teach two science classes in space. The lessons would be beamed live via satellite to classrooms across the country.

4   Beginning in September 1985 McAuliffe, age 37, and the other *Challenger* astronauts, went through 114 hours of space-flight training at the Johnson Space Center in Houston, Texas. Of the other astronauts, all but Jarvis, a civilian engineer, had previously flown on shuttle missions. In 1984 Resnick became the second woman in space. (Sally Ride was the first.) That same year McNair became the second African American to travel in space. Onizuka flew on a secret Defense Department shuttle flight in 1985. Smith, the *Challenger*'s pilot, was one of NASA's most experienced pilots. And Scobee, who had piloted *Challenger* before, was the flight's mission commander.

5   *Challenger*'s **celebrated** launch from Cape Canaveral, Florida, originally was scheduled for January 23, 1986, but bad weather repeatedly postponed the flight. The astronauts remained in quarantine and in good spirits. They relaxed and studied flight plans while they waited in their quarters.

celebrated
famous

6   January 28 was a clear but unusually cold, windy day. In the VIP stands on the roof of Mission Control, the families of the *Challenger* crew shook with **anticipation** and huddled together as the winds blew. As the official countdown began, people across the nation were turning on their televisions. Students were gathered in auditoriums and classrooms to witness the launch. At McAuliffe's school in Concord, New Hampshire, students and faculty were cheering loudly. Some wore party hats and waved noisemakers. **In unison**, they chanted the countdown: "5! 4! 3! 2! 1!"

anticipation
expectation

in unison
together

7   The 11:38 A.M. liftoff was spectacular. Christa McAuliffe's proud parents smiled and hugged each other as *Challenger* cleared the tower. McAuliffe's husband, Steve, and their children, Scott and Caroline, were **jubilant**. It seemed like it would be a great day, but then something went terribly wrong.

jubilant
very joyous and excited

8   One minute and 15 seconds into the flight, Mission Control ordered the shuttle crew: "*Challenger*, go at throttle up." *Challenger*'s pilot followed the command, and the shuttle's engines were thrust into full power. Suddenly the spacecraft erupted into a giant fireball. Initially, spectators assumed the brilliant burst of fire was the separation of the shuttle from its rocket boosters. Seconds later, however, trails of white and orange smoke streaked across the sky. There was silence for approximately 30 seconds, and then Mission Control announced that the shuttle had exploded.

9   The families of the crew members stood motionless in disbelief. McAuliffe's parents hugged but did not move. Jo Ann Jordan, McAuliffe's best friend, cried, "It didn't explode, it didn't explode." All around the country people started to cry. At Concord High School, students stared blankly at the television screen unable to comprehend what had happened. Bonnie Wakeley, a sophomore, said later, "We were watching, and then they were gone. We couldn't believe it."

10   NASA immediately dispatched rescue crews to the crash site about 18 miles offshore. There was a slim chance that the astronauts might be found at sea. Ships and helicopters desperately searched the area to no avail. Later that afternoon, NASA gave the world the horrible news. All of *Challenger*'s crew members perished in the explosion. Rescuers had discovered only chunks of debris in the Atlantic Ocean. However, their search would continue and cover many miles.

Later, in a huge warehouse, NASA investigators sifted through what remained of the 110-ton, $1.2 billion shuttle, searching for clues.

11   The *Challenger* disaster was a devastating setback for NASA and its shuttle program. Thirteen more flights had been scheduled for 1986, but those missions were canceled. McAuliffe's flight would have been the 25th for the shuttle program. In one of her final public statements, she said "I realize there is a risk outside your everyday life, but it doesn't frighten me."

12   Approximately one month after the tragic explosion, search teams located *Challenger*'s cabin and the crew's remains deep in the ocean. NASA was able to determine that the astronauts survived at least several seconds after the explosion. They may have even been alive but unconscious until they struck the ocean's surface.

13   A presidential commission investigated the shuttle disaster for six months. It faulted NASA for allowing the launch to proceed in such cold weather. The 30-degree weather caused a rubber seal between segments of the right rocket booster to fail. Fiery gases then escaped through the defective seal. Like a blowtorch, the hot gases burned through the rocket and ignited the fuel in the shuttle's huge external tank. This created the catastrophic fireball that destroyed the shuttle. A video recording of the flight showed that *Challenger* was in trouble at least 14 seconds prior to the fatal explosion. The crew may have been aware of the impending danger, because a split second before the spaceship exploded, pilot Mike Smith said, "Uh-oh."

14   It would be two and a half years before the United States launched another shuttle. And there would be no immediate plans for another civilian to travel in space.

15   The families of the *Challenger* crew continue to grieve for their loved ones. But in their grief, they carry on *Challenger*'s mission—to educate. The families have praised various projects promoting space exploration and education, and together they founded the Challenger Center for Space Science Education in Virginia. They wanted to have something **dynamic** for children and teachers. "The eyes of those little children who were glued to television—you couldn't just let it end that way, with that terrible loss," said June Scobee, widow of Francis Scobee. "The Challenger Center is a way to talk about how the mission continues…"

dynamic
energetic

Timed Reading

If you have been timed while reading this article, enter your reading time below. Then turn to the Words-per-Minute table on page 129 and look up your reading speed (words per minute). Enter your reading speed on the graph on page 130.

Reading Time: Lesson 3.4

_____ : _____

Minutes   Seconds

Ⓐ Recognize and Recall Details

Put an X next to the phrase that completes each statement.

1. The decision that the first civilian on the space shuttle would be a teacher was announced by

☐ **a.** astronaut Sally Ride.

☐ **b.** President Ronald Reagan.

☐ **c.** Christa McAuliffe.

2. The first woman astronaut to travel in space was

☐ **a.** Judith Resnik.

☐ **b.** Sally Ride.

☐ **c.** Christa McAuliffe.

3. The space shuttle exploded because

☐ **a.** a rubber seal was defective.

☐ **b.** there was too much fuel in the tank.

☐ **c.** the computer system on board failed.

4. During her flight aboard the *Challenger*, Christa McAuliffe planned to

☐ **a.** keep a journal and teach two science classes.

☐ **b.** observe the other astronauts.

☐ **c.** record the technical aspects of spaceflight.

Ⓑ Find the Main Idea

One of the statements below expresses the main idea of the article. One statement is too broad. The other is too narrow—it explains only part of the article. Label the statements using the following key:

M Main Idea	**B** Too Broad	**N** Too Narrow

____ **1.** The launch date for the *Challenger* had been postponed several times because of bad weather.

____ **2.** The space program in the United States slowed down because of the *Challenger* explosion.

____ **3.** People in the United States were stunned when the first shuttle launch to include a private citizen exploded.

C Summarize and Paraphrase

Put an X in the box next to the answer.

1. Complete the following summary of the beginning part of the article:

   After a short introduction, the article about the tragic *Challenger* disaster continues with

   ☐ **a.** a description of Christa McAuliffe's selection and training for the teacher-in-space program.

   ☐ **b.** the causes and effects of the explosion.

   ☐ **c.** the space shuttle's explosion seconds after liftoff.

2. Choose the best paraphrase of the following sentence: "In the VIP stands on the roof of Mission Control, the families of the *Challenger* crew shook with anticipation and huddled together as the winds blew."

   ☐ **a.** The families of the crew members shook with fear as they waited for the *Challenger* to launch.

   ☐ **b.** The families of the crew members clung to each other to keep from being blown off the roof of Mission Control.

   ☐ **c.** The families of the crew members trembled with excitement and pressed close together against the wind as they waited for the *Challenger* launch.

D Make Inferences

The following inferences about the article may or may not be correct. Label the statements using the following key:

C Correct Inference	**F** Faulty Inference

_____ **1.** McAuliffe felt lucky to be chosen the first teacher in space.

_____ **2.** President Reagan thought the space shuttle program was too risky to carry out.

_____ **3.** Despite the disaster, the families of the *Challenger* crew still believe in and support the space program.

_____ **4.** Everyone felt the astronauts would be found alive at sea.

_____ **5.** Because of the *Challenger* disaster, there will never be another chance for a civilian to travel in space.

ⓔ Recognize Author's Effect and Intentions

Put an X in the box next to the answer.

1. The main purpose of the first paragraph is to tell the reader the

   ☐ **a.** names of the crew members who died on *Challenger*.

   ☐ **b.** names of crew members of successful space shuttle flights.

   ☐ **c.** names of several people working for NASA.

2. Which statement from the article best describes Christa McAuliffe's feelings about space exploration?

   ☐ **a.** "She was among 11,000 teachers who submitted applications to NASA."

   ☐ **b.** "McAuliffe went through 114 hours of space-flight training at the Johnson Space Center."

   ☐ **c.** "Ever since childhood, McAuliffe had been fascinated with space."

3. From the statements below, choose the one that you believe the author would agree with.

   ☐ **a.** Christa McAuliffe did not realize that her mission on the Challenger space shuttle could be dangerous.

   ☐ **b.** The decision of NASA officials to launch the Challenger on an unusually cold day was not a factor in the explosion.

   ☐ **c.** After the Challenger disaster, people had a good reason to question NASA's shuttle program.

ⓕ Evaluate and Create

Put an X in the box next to the answer.

1. What was the effect of the *Challenger* disaster on NASA's shuttle program?

   ☐ **a.** NASA founded the Challenger Center for Space Science Education.

   ☐ **b.** Thirteen flights scheduled in 1986 were cancelled.

   ☐ **c.** NASA continued to launch shuttle missions in 1986.

2. Why was the *Challenger* explosion such an intensely human tragedy?

   ☐ **a.** The explosion was a major setback for NASA.

   ☐ **b.** The explosion destroyed a $1.2 billion shuttle.

   ☐ **c.** The explosion killed everyone on board, including the first civilian scheduled to travel in space, while the families of the victims watched.

Oil, Oil Everywhere

The Exxon Baton Rouge *attempts to take crude oil from the Exxon* Valdez. *The* Valdez *ran aground in March 1989, spilling more than 11 million gallons of crude oil. The black gooey substance spread along roughly 1,500 miles of Alaskan coastline.*

Read the title and photo caption and look at the photograph. Think about what you already know about the topic.

Before You Read
Use Background Knowledge

- What major oil-spill disasters have you heard of or read about in the news?

- Based on what you know, how do you think the oil spill affected wildlife in the area?

....

1   Alaska's Prince William Sound is a dazzling jewel in America's last frontier. The jagged coast of the unspoiled sound is dotted with coves and inlets where fish spawn and otters and seals play. Along the shoreline, brown bears catch fish, and deer forage for sea kelp. For years the wildlife and marine life had the beauty of the sound to themselves. Then came the discovery of petroleum.

2   In the 1960s vast reserves of oil were discovered in Prudhoe Bay on Alaska's northern Arctic coast. The state realized that substantial profits could be made by selling oil-drilling leases. It didn't take long for drilling crews to move into the icy, **barren** territory. In the late 1970s an 800-mile pipeline was constructed to carry the thick crude from Prudhoe Bay to the southern port of Valdez. When the oil began to flow, massive ocean-going tankers pulled into the Valdez terminal, loaded their cargo holds, and then proceeded through Prince William Sound.

barren
dry and desolate

3   Environmentalists knew there was the potential for a **catastrophic** oil spill. The state of Alaska and the oil companies who managed the pipeline believed that such a spill in the sound was "highly unlikely," but they grudgingly drafted a cleanup plan. The oil companies said they had complete faith in their tanker pilots.

catastrophic
disastrous

4   Then the unthinkable happened in March 1989, and no one was prepared. It was a tragic example of

Murphy's Law—everything that could go wrong did go wrong.

5   Joseph Hazelwood, captain of the Exxon *Valdez*, had a couple of drinks on shore with shipmates prior to boarding the tanker that Thursday evening. Once inside his cabin, he drank two bottles of low-alcohol beer. The tanker was scheduled to leave the port of Valdez in 45 minutes.

6   Following routine, a harbor pilot came on board to steer the 987-foot tanker out of the port. Approximately two hours later, the harbor pilot departed the ship, and Hazelwood radioed the Coast Guard, saying he would temporarily move the tanker from the outbound shipping lane to the inbound shipping lane to avoid icebergs. He then gave control of the tanker to Third Mate Gregory Cousins. Hazelwood returned to his cabin to complete some paperwork, and for some reason, the Coast Guard ceased monitoring the *Valdez*.

7   Hazelwood had ordered Cousins to make a right turn back into the outbound shipping lane when the vessel reached a point near Busby Island, and Cousins called the captain and told him when he was starting to turn. It would be seven minutes, however, before the *Valdez* actually changed direction, and during this time one of the ship's lookouts spotted something wrong. He raced into the pilothouse and reported that a flashing red buoy near Bligh Reef was on the ship's right (starboard) side when it should have been on the left (port) side. Cousins tried hard to turn the ship, but it was already too late. He picked up the phone, called Hazelwood, and said, "We are in trouble."

impaled
pierced

8   Hazelwood felt the jolt when the *Valdez* **impaled** itself on Bligh Reef. He hurried to the bridge and immediately slowed the engines. He tried to keep

the ship from sliding off the rocky reef and capsizing. Hazelwood knew he couldn't prevent the inevitable—an oil spill in the pristine waters of Prince William Sound—but he did attempt to minimize the size of the disaster.

9   With its side split open, the *Valdez* spewed oil at the rate of 20,000 gallons an hour. Eventually, 11 million gallons would foul the sound. According to the cleanup plan, emergency teams were supposed to arrive on the scene within five hours of the accident. In actuality, it took 10 hours before the first crews arrived. Worse yet, they could do little with their equipment when they did arrive. The oil booms and skimmers were insufficient, and the barge that would carry the skimmed oil was damaged and wasn't operational until the following day. The Coast Guard was equally ill prepared. Its closest cleanup ships were located in San Francisco, 2,000 miles south of Alaska. Many marine animals were already in danger. Ducks were drenched in oil, and sea lions, their flippers coated with crude, were clinging to a buoy near the *Valdez*.

10   As the oil slick snaked through the sound, Exxon Corporation assumed control of the cleanup operation. Local residents, furious and heartsick, accused Exxon of failing to respond quickly enough. They didn't believe Exxon's efforts would protect the fisheries and save the rich wildlife. Commercial fishermen feared the upcoming harvest of salmon and herring would be ruined.

11   Animal rescue centers were overwhelmed with sick, oily animals. Georgia Ruff, a local travel agent, took a leave of absence from her job to volunteer at a center. She learned to wash, dry, feed, and nurse sea otters. The animal's suffering became too much for her to bear. "To hear those animals screaming in pain—it's just awful," Ruff said.

12   The town of Valdez and other nearby villages came close to the breaking point. It was difficult for them to cope with the tragedy and adjust to all the attention from oil company officials, cleanup crews, and the media. In some villages, flags flew at half-staff. Some fishermen wore black armbands; they knew that they would face financial hardships.

13   By mid-May the thick sludge had stained a 1,800-square-mile area. Windy, stormy weather hampered the cleanup operation, which resembled a small army. Crews along the shoreline hosed down the slimy rocks with heated seawater, but progress was extremely slow. The crews had cleaned only 3,300 feet of beach so far, but over 300 miles of oil-covered shoreline remained. On the water the cleanup wasn't any easier. Skimming ships had difficulty pumping the oil from the surface because it was so thick.

requiem
a solemn memorial

14   In a small village called Cordova, saddened townspeople stood in the rain near the waterfront one day and held a **requiem** for Prince William Sound. They could think of little besides the spill. They shared their grief, and wept openly. The oil slick had already killed about 450 otters and almost 3,000 birds.

15   A state environmentalist said, "People are going to have strong feelings about this for a long time. Every time people here go to a favorite fishing hole, they will think of the spill and they will be angry."

16   Exxon fired Captain Hazelwood after receiving the results from his blood-alcohol test. Many felt the company's action came way too late. Exxon knew Hazelwood had a long history of alcohol abuse, and yet it still allowed the captain to maintain his command of the tanker. Hazelwood went to trial a year after the accident, facing felony and several misdemeanor counts. He was convicted of one charge: **negligent**

negligent
careless

discharge of oil. The jury didn't believe that Hazelwood was intoxicated at the time the *Valdez* ran aground.

17 Who was to blame for one of the biggest oil spills in the history of the United States? After a lengthy inquiry, it seems to be mostly Hazelwood, but also the Coast Guard and Exxon. Third Mate Cousins was probably unqualified to steer the *Valdez* through the sound. Captain Hazelwood should have remained at the helm. The Coast Guard should have continued to track the ship by radar. Exxon shouldn't have ignored Hazelwood's drinking problem, and the *Valdez* crew shouldn't have been short staffed and fatigued.

18 Exxon spent billions of dollars to clean Prince William Sound, and it compensated the residents who lost income as a result of the oil spill. The company also vowed to return to pick up where nature's cleaning left off.

19 Four years after the spill, the blackened shoreline was bright again, but otters, ducks, birds, and shellfish were still being poisoned by oil buried in coves. Some who have researched the spill claim it will take decades for Prince William Sound to fully recover.

....

If you have been timed while reading this article, enter your reading time below. Then turn to the Words-per-Minute table on page 129 and look up your reading speed (words per minute). Enter your reading speed on the graph on page 130.

Reading Time: Lesson 3.5

_____ : _____

Minutes   Seconds

Ⓐ Recognize and Recall Details

Put an X in the box next to the answer that completes each statement.

1. In the late 1960s oil was discovered at

☐ **a.** the port of Valdez.

☐ **b.** Prince William Sound.

☐ **c.** Prudhoe Bay.

2. At the time of the accident, the *Valdez* was piloted by

☐ **a.** Joseph Hazelwood.

☐ **b.** a local harbor pilot.

☐ **c.** Gregory Cousins.

3. The side of the *Valdez* was ripped open by

☐ **a.** an iceberg.

☐ **b.** Bligh Reef.

☐ **c.** another tanker.

4. Captain Joseph Hazelwood was eventually convicted of

☐ **a.** all charges.

☐ **b.** negligent discharge of oil.

☐ **c.** alcohol-related charges.

Ⓑ Find the Main Idea

One of the statements below expresses the main idea of the article. One statement is too broad—it is too general. The other statement is too narrow—it explains only part of the article. Label the statements using the following key:

> **M** Main Idea   **B** Too Broad   **N** Too Narrow

____ **1.** One of the worst oil spills in the history of the United States happened in Alaska's Prince William Sound.

____ **2.** Approximately 11 million gallons of oil contaminated the once unspoiled Alaskan coastline.

____ **3.** Although oil companies had drafted cleanup plans, they never thought an oil spill would happen.

C Summarize and Paraphrase

Put an X in the box next to the answer.

1. Choose the summary that says all the most important things about the article in the fewest number of words.

   ☐ **a.** One of the biggest oil spills in the history of the United States occurred when the Exxon *Valdez* impaled itself on Bligh Reef in the pristine waters of Prince William Sound.

   ☐ **b.** The oil spill from the Exxon *Valdez* dumped millions of gallons of crude oil into Prince William Sound, endangering the area's wildlife.

   ☐ **c.** Captain Joseph Hazelwood of the Exxon *Valdez* turned over control of the tanker to Gregory Cousins, who was steering the tanker when it hit Bligh Reef. The tanker began spewing oil.

2. Choose the best reason why the paraphrase does not say the same thing as the statement.

   Statement: The people in the town of Valdez and the other nearby villages had trouble coping with the tragedy and adjusting to the attention from oil company officials, cleanup crews, and the media.

   Paraphrase: After the tragedy of the Exxon *Valdez*, the people in the area had trouble getting the attention of oil company officials, cleanup crews, and the media.

   ☐ **a.** The paraphrase says too much.

   ☐ **b.** The paraphrase doesn't say enough.

   ☐ **c.** The paraphrase doesn't match the statement.

D Make Inferences

The following inferences about the article may or may not be correct. Label the statements using the following key:

C Correct Inference	**F** Faulty Inference

___ **1.** No one who works for an oil company cares about the environment.

___ **2.** Captain Hazelwood is solely responsible for the spill.

___ **3.** Cleanup crews were at fault for not responding sooner.

___ **4.** Surviving animals will probably have more trouble raising their young.

___ **5.** Some people felt that the damage to the environment was too great ever to be repaired.

E Recognize Author's Effect and Intentions

Put an X in the box next to the answer.

1. The main purpose of the first paragraph is to
   - ☐ **a.** encourage the reader to visit Prince William Sound.
   - ☐ **b.** inform the reader about the location of Prince William Sound.
   - ☐ **c.** emphasize the beauty of Prince William Sound.

2. Choose the statement that you believe the author would agree with.
   - ☐ **a.** The people who lived along Prince William Sound were angered by the oil spill only because it would hurt them financially.
   - ☐ **b.** Captain Hazelwood's punishment was too harsh for what he did.
   - ☐ **c.** It will take many years for Prince William Sound to recover from the oil spill.

F Evaluate and Create

Put an X in the box next to the answer.

1. Judging from Joseph Hazelwood's actions, you can predict that
   - ☐ **a.** the captain would become a commercial airline pilot.
   - ☐ **b.** Exxon would rehire the captain after a few years' probation.
   - ☐ **c.** he would never again be captain of an oil tanker.

2. Choose from the letters below to correctly complete the following statement: In the article, Captain Hazelwood and _____ play a similar role in the events leading up to the oil spill.
   - ☐ **a.** state environmentalists
   - ☐ **b.** the fishermen
   - ☐ **c.** Gregory Cousins

3. If you were an oil company official, how could you use the information in the article to draft a cleanup plan in case of a future oil spill?
   - ☐ **a.** Make sure that emergency teams understand their jobs and insist that the Coast Guard monitor tankers.
   - ☐ **b.** Assure the people living in the area that a catastrophic spill is highly unlikely.
   - ☐ **c.** Allow time and nature to take care of most of the cleanup.

WORDS-PER-MINUTE TABLE

Directions If you were timed while reading an article, refer to the reading time you recorded at the end of the article. Use this Words-per-Minute table to determine your reading speed for that article. Then plot your reading speed on the graph on page 130.

Lesson	1.1	1.2	1.3	1.4	1.5	2.1	2.2	2.3	2.4	2.5	3.1	3.2	3.3	3.4	3.5	
No. of Words	1462	1386	843	1182	1117	866	1075	1235	1509	802	881	1485	1027	1101	1303	
1:30	975	924	562	788	745	577	717	823	1006	535	587	990	685	734	869	90
1:40	877	832	506	709	670	520	645	741	905	481	529	891	616	661	782	100
1:50	797	756	460	645	609	472	586	674	823	437	481	810	560	601	711	110
2:00	731	693	422	591	559	433	538	618	755	401	441	743	514	551	652	120
2:10	675	640	389	546	516	400	496	570	696	370	407	685	474	508	601	130
2:20	627	594	361	507	479	371	461	529	647	344	378	636	440	472	558	140
2:30	585	554	337	473	447	346	430	494	604	321	352	594	411	440	521	150
2:40	548	520	316	443	419	325	403	463	566	301	330	557	385	413	489	160
2:50	516	489	298	417	394	306	379	436	533	283	311	524	362	389	460	170
3:00	487	462	281	394	372	289	358	412	503	267	294	495	342	367	434	180
3:10	462	438	266	373	353	273	339	390	477	253	278	469	324	348	411	190
3:20	439	416	253	355	335	260	323	371	453	241	264	446	308	330	391	200
3:30	418	396	241	338	319	247	307	353	431	229	252	424	293	315	372	210
3:40	399	378	230	322	305	236	293	337	412	219	240	405	280	300	355	220
3:50	381	362	220	308	291	226	280	322	394	209	230	387	268	287	340	230
4:00	366	347	211	296	279	217	269	309	377	201	220	371	257	275	326	240
4:10	351	333	202	284	268	208	258	296	362	192	211	356	246	264	313	250
4:20	337	320	195	273	258	200	248	285	348	185	203	343	237	254	301	260
4:30	325	308	187	263	248	192	239	274	335	178	196	330	228	245	290	270
4:40	313	297	181	253	239	186	230	265	323	172	189	318	220	236	279	280
4:50	302	287	174	245	231	179	222	256	312	166	182	307	212	228	270	290
5:00	292	277	169	236	223	173	215	247	302	160	176	297	205	220	261	300
5:10	283	268	163	229	216	168	208	239	292	155	171	287	199	213	252	310
5:20	274	260	158	222	209	162	202	232	283	150	165	278	193	206	244	320
5:30	266	252	153	215	203	157	195	225	274	146	160	270	187	200	237	330
5:40	258	245	149	209	197	153	190	218	266	142	155	262	181	194	230	340
5:50	251	238	145	203	191	148	184	212	259	137	151	255	176	189	223	350
6:00	244	231	141	197	186	144	179	206	252	134	147	248	171	184	217	360
6:10	237	225	137	192	181	140	174	200	245	130	143	241	167	179	211	370
6:20	231	219	133	187	176	137	170	195	238	127	139	234	162	174	206	380
6:30	225	213	130	182	172	133	165	190	232	123	136	228	158	169	200	390
6:40	219	208	126	177	168	130	161	185	226	120	132	223	154	165	195	400
6:50	214	203	123	173	163	127	157	181	221	117	129	217	150	161	191	410
7:00	209	198	120	169	160	124	154	176	216	115	126	212	147	157	186	420
7:10	204	193	118	165	156	121	150	172	211	112	123	207	143	154	182	430
7:20	199	189	115	161	152	118	147	168	206	109	120	203	140	150	178	440
7:30	195	185	112	158	149	115	143	165	201	107	117	198	137	147	174	450
7:40	191	181	110	154	146	113	140	161	197	105	115	194	134	144	170	460
7:50	187	177	108	151	143	111	137	158	193	102	112	190	131	141	166	470
8:00	183	173	105	148	140	108	134	154	189	100	110	186	128	138	163	480

Minutes and Seconds

Seconds

PLOTTING YOUR PROGRESS GRAPH: READING SPEED

Directions If you were timed while reading an article, find your reading speed on the Words-per-Minute table. Then plot your reading speed on this graph by putting a small X on the line directly above the number of the lesson, across from the number of words per minute you read. As you mark your speed for each lesson, graph your progress by drawing a line to connect the Xs.

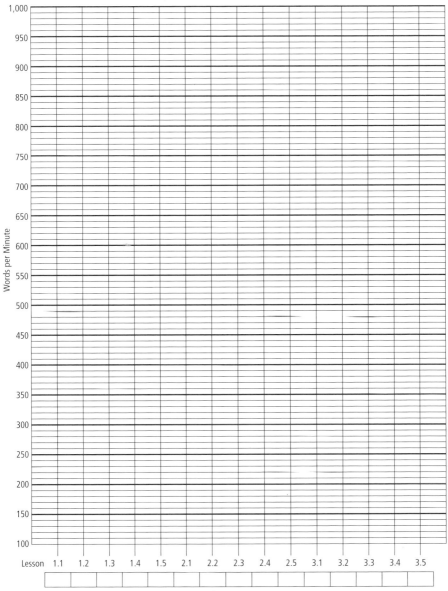

Words-per-Minute Score